HANGING BASKETS, WINDOW BOXES, AND OTHER CONTAINER GARDENS

HANGING BASKETS, WINDOW BOXES, AND OTHER CONTAINER GARDENS

A GUIDE TO CREATIVE SMALL-SCALE GARDENING

DAVID JOYCE

NEW YORK LONDON TORONTO SYDNEY TOKYO SINGAPORE

Page 1: A grape vine and shutters frame pots of busy lizzies *(Impatiens)* and a window box of nasturtiums *(Tropaeloum majus)* and petunias.

Page 2: Summer flowers, especially pelargoniums, in a variety of containers are co-ordinated to dress the front of this building.

Right: Bright petunias and zonal pelargoniums are a match for a trough that adds a touch of colorful domesticity to this barge.

SIMON & SCHUSTER

Simon & Schuster Building
Rockefeller Center
1230 Avenue of the Americas
New York, New York 10020

Text copyright © 1991 by David Joyce

First published in 1991 by
Conran Octopus Limited
37 Shelton Street, London WC2H 9HN

Simon & Schuster and colophon are trademarks of Simon & Schuster Inc.
Formerly published by Summit Books

Printed in China

10 9 8 7 6

Library of Congress Cataloging-in-Publication Data
Joyce, David.
    Hanging baskets, window boxes, and other container gardens: a guide to decorative small-scale gardening/ David Joyce.
        p.   cm.
    Includes index.
    ISBN 0-671-74440-2
    1. Container gardening. 2. Container gardening – Pictorial works.
    1. Title
SB418.J69 1992   90-28911
635.9'86–dc20   CIP

CONTENTS

INTRODUCTION 6

FOUR-SEASON GARDENING 10

GARDENING TECHNIQUES 22

HANGING BASKETS 32

WINDOW BOXES 48

OTHER CONTAINERS 62

PLANT DIRECTORY 84

INDEX 94

ACKNOWLEDGMENTS 96

INTRODUCTION

Since very early times gardeners have had the idea of growing plants in containers. The practice may have begun as a way of nurturing treasured rarities or plants charged with a special religious or mystical significance. Old frescoes and paintings provide ample evidence, though, that the decorative value of container-grown plants has been appreciated for a very long time.

Much in container gardening has remained unchanged over many centuries. We still grow plants that were loved by gardeners hundreds of years ago and containers of traditional designs and materials continue to be widely used. There have been changes, however, particularly with the extraordinary expansion of gardening as a leisure activity over the last 50 years. New materials, such as fiberglass and plastics, have been used in the manufacture of a greatly increased range of containers. The hanging basket, already known to the Victorians, has come into its own. Furthermore, the transformation of the retail trade means that it is easy to buy all the supplies needed for the container garden – from the pots and hanging baskets themselves to plants suitable for growing in them – at garden centers and other outlets.

Colorful half-hardy plants give a long summer display and do well in all kinds of containers. The hanging baskets contain petunias, lobelias, fuchsias, pelargoniums and a gray-leaved foliage plant which cools the hotter tones. In the window boxes are petunias and lobelias.

Above : Hardy annuals and biennials include some of the most dependably free-flowering plants for all kinds of containers. Pansies, which are really short-lived perennials, are normally grown as annuals. 'Coronation Gold' is here used on its own but pansies mix well with other plants.

Top, left : There are bulbs for every month of the year but it is spring bulbs such as daffodils that make the greatest impact.

Bottom, left : *Osteospermum ecklonis* is one of a number of long-flowering perennials which are suitable for container planting but need protection to survive a cold winter.

Opposite : The choice among shrubs for containers includes deciduous and evergreen kinds, some grown mainly for their flowers and others, such as these clipped box (*Buxus*), for their foliage.

PLANTS FOR CONTAINERS

Introductions from the wild and a long history of breeding provide a wide choice of plants to fill the containers we choose. A selection, belonging to the main groups described below, is given on pages 84-93.

The longest lived are the woody plants, trees and shrubs. Trees and larger shrubs need very big containers but there are also many superlative shrubs of medium or short stature, some valued particularly for their flowers and others for foliage. Roses are an important group of shrubs that has been much worked on by breeders. There are so many cultivars that roses are generally treated as a category of ornamentals on their own.

Herbaceous perennials are generally thought of as long-term plants for the open garden. However, many adapt well to life in containers, including good foliage and flowering plants. More tender ones, such as begonias, can be grown as annuals but can be kept through the winter if protected from frost, for example in a greenhouse.

Bulbs (the term is here used loosely to include corms and tubers) are a special group of perennials that deserve separate treatment. They are indispensable for spring and include numerous star performers for other seasons.

Three main groups of short-lived ornamentals are the mainstay of many container gardens. The first are biennials, plants that flower and then die the year after they have been sown. Wallflowers (*Cheiranthus cheiri*), which are representative of this group, are generally bought as plants in early spring, although the gardener can sow his own seeds in summer for flowers the following spring. Annuals, plants that complete their life cycle in a season, fall into two categories. Hardy annuals, such as cosmos and pot marigolds (*Calendula*) are easily grown from seed sown in spring. Half-hardy annuals, like french marigolds (*Tagetes*), are best started in heat in spring and many gardeners prefer to buy commercially raised stock of these.

Useful plants are also often decorative and in the container garden there is room for herbs and even vegetables and fruit.

FOUR-SEASON GARDENING

A bumper planting for summer preceded sometimes by a modest scheme for spring, mainly of bulbs potted up in the autumn, is still a common pattern in container gardening. There is, however, no reason why gardening on a small scale should ignore the full sweep of the seasons. It is, after all, the marked change of the seasons that gives gardening in the temperate world a drama and excitement that can sometimes seem sadly lacking in the tropics.

Your emphasis may not be the same throughout the whole year. Flower color may be all important in summer and at this time, for the best effects, you should consider carefully how to handle a palette of potentially overwhelming brilliance. Foliage may help solve the problem of competing colors and it may provide the theme for year-round planting. At quieter times of the year you may prefer to change the focus, moving into detail instead of aiming to create broad effects. Old hands will tell you that there is no sweeter delight than having plant treasures for every month of the year. Whatever approach you adopt, the key to success is choosing the right plant for the right place and giving plants conditions for optimum growth.

Winter frost highlights the shapes of box (*Buxus*) topiary against hedges of evergreen conifers. Clipped bay trees (*Laurus nobilis*) and hollies (*Ilex*) also make excellent container subjects for a formal effect. All need trimming at least once a year to keep their shape.

PLANNING FOR THE OFF-SEASON

The period from the end of summer until early spring is undoubtedly the leanest time of the year in the garden. Some people mistakenly think it is so lean that they give up all expectation of pleasure from plants and turn their backs on the container garden. But even in the darkest weeks of the year there are some plants that are at their best or are at least performing just as reliably and effectively as at the height of summer. Many of the plants that give off-season value are no more demanding than familiar plants of the peak season.

In autumn, berrying shrubs such as pernettyas and skimmias strike the right seasonal note as do a few deciduous shrubs with good autumn colors, especially Japanese maples (*Acer palmatum*).

Evergreens, such as ivy (*Hedera* species), box (*Buxus sempervirens*) and some of the dwarf conifers, among them cultivars of *Chamaecyparis* and *Thuja*, stalwarts throughout the year, come into their own as autumn advances. The many shades of green extend into blues, grays and golds, not to mention variegations from cream to deep yellow. Some evergreens, box in particular, respond well to trimming and for me the severe geometry or fanciful shapes of topiary are never more appealing than in winter.

Among evergreens that grow in warm climates are a few herbaceous plants. Some, such as bergenias and heucheras, have been made popular as ground-cover plants but there is scope for more of them in containers, especially to fill winter gaps.

Top of my list for flowering plants in the lean seasons are bulbs. Many are easy to grow and, although the flowers seem delicate, they stand up to rough weather surprisingly well. Outstanding among them are species crocuses, cyclamen, grape hyacinths (*Muscari*), dwarf irises, scillas and snowdrops (*Galanthus*). Even some of the earliest daffodils and tulips can brighten the last few weeks of winter and early spring. Most of the early bulbs are short in stature and suitable for window boxes, troughs and similar containers.

Good shrubs that do well in containers and flower in winter and early spring include Japanese

quince (*Chaenomeles*), camellias, among them deep pink 'Anticipation' and rosy pink 'St Ewe', and the first rhododendrons, such as *R.* × *cilpinense* with bell-shaped pink flowers. On a much smaller scale there are the long-lasting winter-flowering heaths (some of the many *Erica carnea* and *E.* × *darleyensis* cultivars).

What the container garden lacks between autumn and early spring are the showy flowers that are the glory of high spring and summer. To some extent the gap is filled by a few dazzling performers that cover a wide color range. The early-flowering pansies are exceptionally good value and offer one of the best solutions to planting a hanging basket in the off-season period. The primula family also includes early-flowering plants, the most colorful of which are the popular polyanthus. If you find their form and color exaggerated, look out for more refined primrose-like hybrids. Another plant to consider is the English daisy (*Bellis perennis*), the cultivated forms

Opposite: Pelargoniums (popularly known as bedding geraniums) are not hardy but they are first-rate and easygoing container plants, with a long summer-flowering season if they are dead-headed regularly.

Above: Bulbs are indispensable spring flowers, alone or in combinations, as these tulips mixed with forget-me-nots show. There are both species and cultivars of tulips, such as this 'West Point', that have starry flowers and pointed petals.

of which have flowers in colors ranging from white, through pink to crimson.

It would be odd if we did not look forward to the massed flowers of spring and summer. For myself, though, I am glad to see the seasons change and I enjoy with a special pleasure the flowers of the darkest months, quieter but no less beautiful than the colorful flowers of summer.

FLOWER COLOR

Plant breeders have developed bright, large-bloomed and long-lasting flowers that are just the thing for hanging baskets and other containers. The palette, it has to be admitted, is very strong and on a limited canvas it can be overwhelming. The patio or balcony garden dazzling with feverish luminosity is an effect that is all too easily achieved.

One can admire the vitality of random mixtures and bold experimentation while falling back with relief on more conventional color combinations. Actually these are rarely quite as conventional as they seem, for there are complex nuances and subtle combinations of color within each flower.

A combination of the complementary colors blue and yellow is a good basis for both spring and summer plantings. There are many small blue-flowered bulbs to go with daffodils and there are several variations to play on yellow tulips, blue and yellow hyacinths, blue pansies and forget-me-nots (*Myosotis*). To give a wider range of options the yellows can be extended to near whites on the one hand and to reddish tones on the other. In summer, campanulas, *Felicia amelloides,* the ever-popular lobelia and blue or purplish petunias go well with sunny plants such as pot marigolds (*Calendula officinalis*), nasturtiums, and yellow pansies and petunias.

Left: A planting of *Ageratum*, ivy-leaved and zonal pelargoniums, lobelias and red mimulus, is the basis of a restrained scheme in whites, blues and pinks. The gray-leaved *Helichrysum* sustains the muted color theme.

Opposite: The bold statement made by a dense planting of flowers in a single color can be particularly effective in spring. Here a handsome oriental *jardinière* has been planted with grape hyacinths (*Muscari*). Their vivid blue stands out well on its own but would also work successfully with yellow, the dominant color of the first half of spring. The planting has more to it than first meets the eye. Short-growing tulips are beginning to push through the grape hyacinths.

Above: The English ivy (*Hedera helix*) is one of the most versatile foliage plants for all kinds of containers, its numerous cultivars showing great differences in leaf shape and color. It is evergreen and the variegated and golden forms give a year-round display of bright trailing foliage.

Right : Foliage plants such as ivy (*Hedera helix*) are valuable companions to flowering plants in containers. They give fullness to the planting, soften hard outlines and provide a background to flowers. A standard large-flowered single fuchsia is here underplanted with ivy and other single- and double-flowered fuchsias.

Another good combination, especially for a summer display, is based on blues, pinks and mauves. The blues already mentioned mix well with fuchsias, pelargoniums and verbenas and a touch of white can add a note of distinction and lighten the effect.

Variations on a single color can also be highly successful, although often the beauty of these combinations is enhanced by the hint of another color. White marguerites, such as 'Chelsea Girl', and petunias make a lovely cool combination but a little blue or purple, perhaps from a verbena, such as 'Cupido', gives an added depth.

Variations on hotter colors can also work well, although generally they are more difficult to carry off and sometimes the best way of handling plants that produce big fleshy flowers in strong, vibrant reds and oranges, such as begonias, is to plant them separately.

FLOWERS AND FOLIAGE

Many of the problems presented by strongly colored and densely flowering plants can be solved by combining them with good foliage plants. When well chosen, these act as a foil for flower color and even as peacemakers, helping to calm mixtures of color that might otherwise seem ill-matched and garish.

In foliage itself there is a very wide range of colors and there are also interesting differences of texture and leaf size. The English ivy (*Hedera helix*), for example, has an extraordinarily wide range of forms, varying considerably in leaf size and shape as well as in color. There are solid shades from deep greens ('Digitata') to creamy yellow ('Buttercup') and variegations extend from icy white ('Glacier') to buttery gold ('Goldheart'). Ivy thoroughly deserves its popularity as an all-season foliage plant. One of the most useful foliage plants for mixed summer displays is the tender *Helichrysum petiolatum,* which has a lightly variegated form, 'Variegatum', and a pale creamy form, 'Limelight'. Both of these help lighten the effect of dense and rich plantings.

Foliage, of course, is not just a color component

in a mixture. It also gives body to a combination of plants, especially when straying tendrils suggest surging growth. And it sustains the planting so that even when there is a lull in flowering the mixture looks respectable. The subtle foliage planting of the kind that is increasingly common in gardens, in which texture and leaf shape play an important part, also shows that foliage can be made the main feature of a container planting scheme. A variegated *Agave* (*A. americana* 'Variegata') or a handsome gray-leaved plant, for example *Senecio maritima* 'Cirrus', could be made the centerpieces of large containers with a few flowering companion plants softening the edges of the pot. The finest foliage plants, which include Japanese maples, dwarf conifers, hostas, ferns and grasses, need no flowers to "prettify" them and make splendid isolated specimens in their own right, although they are useful as focal points in a grouping of planted containers. In summer, for instance, a bay tree (*Laurus nobilis*) which has been trained as a standard makes a striking centerpiece.

Above: Many favorite plants of container gardening give a long display of densely packed flowers in vibrant colors. The greens and cooling creams and grays of foliage plants help to dilute what can all too easily prove to be overpoweringly colorful. Unlike the foliage of many flowering plants, the shiny green leaves of ivy-leaved pelargoniums, here grown in a bold combination of pink and red, are an effective foil for the bright flowers.

RIGHT PLANT, RIGHT PLACE

Container gardening is one of the easiest ways to provide growing conditions that suit the needs of specific plants. The growing medium can be adjusted to suit their requirements and the containers themselves can be moved about.

Sun and shade

Most gardening in containers is done near buildings and architecture creates sharply divided zones of sun and shade that shift throughout the day and also through the seasons. Near buildings it is rare to have a graduated zone of dappled light gently filtered by overhanging foliage, as there often is in the open garden.

A practical step which can be taken to increase the amount of light in shady areas is to paint walls white. A more adventurous approach is to use mirrors, which reflect light and also give an illusion of space.

In cool temperature climates, as in the Pacific Northwest, to have an area for container gardening that enjoys full sun seems exceptional good fortune. The drawback is that when the sun really shines containers can dry out very quickly. In hot weather a hanging basket exposed to full sun may need watering several times a day.

In many ways an area that gets some shade while catching the sun in summer for at least half the day is ideal. Most sun-loving plants, such as petunias and verbenas, will do well in these situations, although they tend to produce slightly fewer flowers and more leaf growth than they would in optimum conditions. If you have sunny and shady areas, it can be worth ringing the changes on your arrangement of containers. Many plants that like full sun will quite happily tolerate a few days in shade.

The real solution for shade, however, is to grow plants that like it. These can be flowering plants, such as camellias (which have handsome glossy foliage when out of flower) and busy lizzies (*Impatiens*). There are good foliage plants, too, including evergreens, such as box and ivy, and herbaceous perennials, such as ferns and hostas.

Left : Many plants suitable for container gardening will flourish in partial shade, and this is especially true of foliage plants such as bergenias, hostas and ferns. Outstanding among flowering annuals for shade are the busy lizzies (*Impatiens*), which give a long and full display. Here they are grown in hanging baskets and other containers, their glowing colors brightening a cool retreat.

Above : Many half-hardy and hardy annuals need a sunny position if they are to flower freely. Where the position is too shady they make lank leafy growth and produce few flowers. Nemesias, here growing with lobelias, are typical sun lovers. They are available in a wide range of colors, including blue, and will give a second flush of flowers if cut back as soon as the first flush is over.

Wind and turbulence

Container-grown plants are particularly vulnerable to wind damage because of their exposed position, and the higher above ground they are the more vulnerable they become. The containers themselves also suffer damage in strong winds and can topple over, particularly if they have top-heavy plantings with dense foliage.

For exposed positions it is essential to choose sturdy plants of short stature. Tall daffodils and tulips in window boxes invite disaster but short-growing daffodils such as 'Jack Snipe' and 'Tête-à-Tête' and tulips such as the pink 'Heart's Delight' and the red and salmon 'Shakespeare', will stand up to spring squalls. Many popular plants are available in a range that includes compact cultivars and hybrids and in general these are the ones best suited to growing in containers.

Left: When acid-loving plants are grown in alkaline soil they become sickly and eventually succumb, but they are easily grown in containers using an acid potting medium, often sold as an ericaceous mixture. Camellias and rhododendrons belong to this group, as do the species and cultivars of *Pieris*. Several *Pieris*, such as this *P. formosa* var. *forrestii*, make new growth in spring of a wonderfully rich red fading to pink.

Opposite, top : A shallow stone trough makes a lovely container for miniatures but because it can only hold a small amount of soil it is best used for plants that enjoy free-draining conditions and are reasonably tolerant of drought. This example of an old stone sink has been planted with dwarf sedums and sempervivums.

Opposite, bottom : In hot summers pots containing moisture-loving plants may need to be watered several times a day but plants that can be grown in shade will not dry out so quickly. Ferns, hostas, tolmiea, miniature bamboos and other foliage plants, as in this collection, need regular watering but will thrive even where the shade is quite heavy.

Dry and moist conditions

Some plants are much more tolerant of dry soils than others. To some extent adjustments to the potting medium can help to meet a plant's requirements for moisture (the range of media suitable for container-grown plants is summarized on page 24). But there are other factors to take into account. Exposure to sun and wind speeds up water evaporation, so plants which can be grown in shaded, sheltered positions will retain moisture for longer. The size of a container and the material of which it is made are relevant. A smaller container will obviously hold less potting mix, and therefore need watering more frequently, and potting mix in terracotta dries out more quickly than in plastic containers.

The number of plants competing for the water supply is also important. Water loss can be slowed down by a mulch, for example of coarse grit, spread as a surface layer over the potting mix. Recent developments include experiments with water-absorbent gels that can be added to potting mixes. But, in principle, if you cannot water containers regularly, it is wise to keep to relatively drought-resistant plants including some herbs such as thyme and sage, and the succulent semper-vivums and sedums.

Acid and alkaline preferences

Camellias and rhododendrons are among a number of plants that will not thrive in alkaline (limy) soils. Although it may not be possible to satisfy them in the open garden, this is one of the areas where containers have a positive advantage, for they can be grown in containers filled with a suitably acid medium. An ordinary medium will not do, for most contain some lime, which is alkaline. What is needed is a special mixture for acid lovers, sometimes called an ericaceous mixture. I would not want to flaunt a container-grown rhododendron in the heart of an open garden on chalk, where it would seem too much at odds with the environment. But in a little courtyard or on a terrace where the setting was formal I would have no scruples.

GARDENING
TECHNIQUES

The title of this section risks putting some people off an activity that does not in fact require profound scientific knowledge or elaborate equipment to give an enormous amount of pleasure. It is useful, however, to have a section in a book devoted to gardening in containers that summarizes useful practical information, even though much of it is actually simple common sense. The information gathered here is intended as a quick reference. Some of the points, particularly on planting up containers, are made again more forcefully by the illustrated step-by-step sequences that occur throughout the book.

The care and management of plants in containers is essentially the same as for plants in the open garden, but it has to be admitted that in some ways the container gardener has to be more vigilant. This is particularly so when it comes to watering. Unless the gardener sees to it that plants in containers get an adequate and regular supply of water, only the toughest and most drought-resistant plants will stand a chance of survival. With reasonably careful management, however, there is almost no limit to the range of plants that can be grown.

Very little specialized equipment is needed at any stage in the growing of plants in containers. The kitchen table generally provides a perfectly satisfactory substitute for the potting bench, shown here with potting medium, crocks and plants, including violas, ready to pot on.

23

Below: Soil-based potting mixes have advantages over soil-less kinds for shrubs. Their nutrients last longer and provide a firmer anchor, useful here for the ivy arch as well as the box.

CHOOSING AND MAKING POTTING MIXES

Although plants in the open garden may do well in ordinary soil, it is generally not a satisfactory growing medium in containers. It may harbor pests and diseases; it may contain weeds or weed seeds; and there can also be a lack of some nutrients and even an excess of others. The ideal medium for most container-grown plants is a sterile mixture that is free-draining but also reasonably water-retentive and contains a well-balanced supply of the principal minerals required for plant growth – nitrogen, phosphorus and potassium – and essential trace elements. For many gardeners the commercially prepared mixtures which come readily available in manageable pre-packed quantities from garden centers and other outlets are the most convenient to use.

Potting mixtures fall into two main groups: soil-based mixes and soil-less media. Soil-based mixes may be made with pasteurized garden loam or commercial potting soil. Some potting soils contain fertilizers, but it is better to buy the kind that contains no fertilizer and add your own. Other ingredients for potting mixes are perlite, vermiculite, peat moss and builder's sand. Organic gardeners like to add compost to their potting mixes, and many gardeners also add a tablespoon of bonemeal for each quart of potting medium. Although many commercial potting soils contain some perlite or vermiculite and peat, and are sold as ready-to-use planting mixtures, they often contain too high a proportion of soil and are thus too heavy and dense to use by themselves. Most gardeners therefore choose to add additional peat, perlite, or vermiculite in order to lighten and improve the texture.

The second main category of potting mixes is soil-less media, which are usually made of peat, perlite and vermiculite blended in varying proportions. Soil-less propagation mixes are especially useful, and are sold by many garden centers, nurseries and mail-order seed companies. Steril-ized soil-less media are generally preferred for starting seeds and rooting cuttings because they minimize the risk of damping-off and other fungus diseases. One of the most popular of these propagation media, used by professional horticul-turists and home gardeners alike, is Pro-Mix, a blend of equal parts of peat moss and perlite. Special peat-based potting mixes are also used for ericaceous and other acid-loving plants such as camellias and azaleas.

There is growing concern that the commercial exploitation of peat reserves is causing irreversible environmental damage. But because there are limited supplies of good-quality loam, soil-less media will continue to be widely used in the near future. We can nevertheless expect to see an increasing range of materials substituted for peat. One of the most promising to date is coir, the fibrous husk of the coconut.

Among the merits of soil-based media is the fact that their nutrients are not exhausted as quickly as those in other mixes and they are therefore particularly suitable for long-term planting of shrubs. They are also much better at anchoring trees, shrubs and other top-heavy plants. However, their weight counts against them in hanging baskets, window boxes and any container that needs lifting or supporting. For general ease of handling the soil-less mixes are difficult to beat. Their great disadvantage, in addition to the environmental black mark against using peat-based potting mixes is that, although they are fairly water retentive, once they dry out they are very difficult to wet again.

The standard mixtures, either loam-based or peat-based, can be varied to suit the requirements of certain plants, especially those, such as many of the miniatures suitable for sinks, that like very free drainage. If coarse sand is to be added to increase drainage, remember that it will mix more readily when it is dry.

Many gardeners make up their own mixes, the principal difficulty being the sterilization of the ingredients. It is possible to buy sterilizing equip-ment but for small quantities the simplest method is heat treatment for several hours in an oven. If you are making up your own mixes, it is worth trying to use alternatives to peat.

Most experienced gardeners develop their own recipes for potting mixes over the course of their gardening lives. Blending one's own potting media affords the opportunity to adjust the proportions of the ingredients according to plants' needs. Extra peat moss can be added for acid-loving plants, or lime can be added for plants that prefer neutral or slightly alkaline soil. One good soil-based mix can be made with two parts of soil and one part each of perlite or vermiculite and peat moss or leaf mold. A classic soil-less potting medium for either indoor or outdoor plants is equal parts of peat, perlite, and vermiculite. One tablespoon of bonemeal can be added to each quart of either of these mixtures if you choose.

BUYING PLANTS

Summer bedding plants that are suitable for containers, such as petunias and verbenas, are readily available as young stock in spring, often grown in individual pots, and also in strips or in trays. Plants potted individually can be very expensive and are not necessarily a better buy than other stock available from garden centers. What is most important is to check that plants are vigorous and healthy and have suffered no checks to their growth, for example through lack of water or as a result of the nutrients in their potting mix being exhausted.

Below: Rhododendrons are a major group of plants that need an acid potting mix. The pot containing this magnificent *R.* 'Hinomayo' is tied to its base to prevent it from toppling.

Signs that warn of plants having suffered neglect include competition from weeds, yellowing leaves, stunted or lanky growth, dry soil and limp foliage. Plants that have been in their containers too long may have roots showing through the bottom. Remember always to check for signs of pests and diseases, and in particular look at young shoots and the underside of young leaves to make sure that there is no infestation of aphids, such as greenfly, as these are the virus carriers and once a plant has a virus it cannot be cured. The plants you choose should be bushy, with fresh growth and plenty of young shoots and flower buds. A few flowers already out is not a bad sign but reject plants that carry numerous faded blooms.

There is a good chance that plants available in mid- to late spring, which will have been germinated and grown in moderate heat, have not been fully accustomed to the cooler conditions outdoors. Certainly there will be half-hardy plants on offer long before the risk of frost is over. Making sure that plants are properly hardened off (see GROWING PLANTS FROM SEED, page 27) and ready to go outdoors is an important point to bear in mind when planting. It is often easier to harden plants off as bought and to plant up a couple of weeks later rather than struggling against the odds to protect fully planted hanging baskets or window boxes from frost.

Biennials such as sweet williams (*Dianthus barbatus*) and wall flowers (*Cheiranthus cheiri*) are also offered for sale in spring. For best results buy stock as soon as it becomes available and reject limp plants with yellowing leaves. If at all possible, plant immediately after you get the plants home. When there is a delay between purchase and planting, you must always remember to keep the plants moist, and put them in a cool, lightly shaded and sheltered place.

Most perennials are now sold as container-grown stock, which can be planted in spring or autumn, provided that watering is not neglected. Many nurseries and garden centers are geared to a selling peak in spring and more traditional ones to an autumn planting season as well. During the plant's dormant season you cannot judge a plant by the quality of its foliage but you should be able to see new growth buds just above or just below the surface of the soil.

Reject plants that are in weed-filled pots and any where the roots have grown out of the pot (lift the pot up and look underneath) or where the roots have formed a choking spiral in the container. By gently probing the soil with your fingers you can get an idea of whether a plant is root bound.

Most shrubs are also now sold as container-grown specimens and can be bought and replanted in spring or autumn. However, some large shrubs and young trees are sold with bare roots and others ball-rooted, that is with soil around the roots which is held in by a covering of burlap. Bare-rooted and ball-rooted specimens should only be bought and planted during the dormant season, that is, in late winter or early spring, depending on your location.

When buying shrubs, select specimens that are well proportioned and free of signs of damage, disease or pest infestation. Weeds on the surface of a container can indicate that a plant has been in its pot too long and has suffered checks to its growth through competition for water and nutrients. Pot-bound plants, with roots emerging from the base of the container or pushing up the sides, should be rejected.

Sometimes plants in containers have not been container-grown but lifted from open ground in autumn and put in a pot that is then filled with soil. When plants have been containerized in this way, labelling should make this clear but often it does not. Plants such as roses that have been contain-erized can be perfectly satisfactory if they are bought and replanted in the dormant period, but stock should not be carried over past the following spring. When buying plants, be sure to ask whether they have been container-grown or containerized. If you are still in doubt, pull lightly at the main stem. The stem and roots of plants that have only been containerized will generally come away quite easily from the soil.

Hardy bulbs are rarely available before late summer and it may be well into autumn before there are stocks of some lilies. Buy as early as possible to get the widest choice and while bulbs are still in good condition (many shrivel quite quickly where central heating creates a warm dry atmosphere). Whenever possible, select your own bulbs, choosing healthy plump specimens and discarding those that are damaged, shrivelled or show symptoms of rot. In general, hardy bulbs should be planted in autumn, at least a month before the ground freezes so they have time to establish roots in the soil. If bulbs are stored, they should be kept in a cool dark place. Gardeners in warm climates must refrigerate bulbs for several weeks before planting, to give them the necessary cold period.

The tubers of the tender *Begonia × tuberhy-brida* and other summer-flowering bulbous plants that are not fully hardy are generally available in spring; plant when the danger of frost is past.

Above, left: The cheapest, and for many gardeners the most enjoyable, way to obtain stocks of plants is to raise them from seed. Several ornamentals, including nasturtiums and sweet peas, and vegetables – those shown here are runner beans (brown) and peas (white) – have large seeds that are easily handled. The seeds can be spaced out individually in pots or trays of seed-starting medium and pressed in until covered to just over their own depth by the medium. Finer seeds must be sprinkled thinly and evenly and then lightly covered with medium or, if very fine, simply left on the surface.

Above, right: Annuals, such as beans (top and bottom) and peas (two middle pots), germinate quickly, sometimes within a matter of days, but some herbaceous perennials and many trees and shrubs may take months, even more than a year, to show their first leaves.

GROWING PLANTS FROM SEED

For many gardeners the pleasure of growing plants is not complete unless they have raised their own stock and starting from seed is a relatively inexpensive way of getting a good number of plants. While it is true that there are plants that are difficult to germinate and slow to reach maturity when grown from seed – this is especially so for some trees – there are other plants that are easy even for the inexperienced gardener. The most satisfying for container gardens are generally hardy and half-hardy annuals, plants that will flower in the same year as they are sown. Their rapid growth means that they do not take up a lot of space before they are ready to be planted into containers. By starting them early, in warm conditions such as a heated greenhouse, even on a kitchen window sill or in a glassed porch, they will give you a long flowering season. Biennials and some perennials are also easy but, for the gardener who does not have open ground in which they can be grown on, they can unfortunately take up too much room before they are ready to plant out for flowering.

Seed of annuals and biennials can be collected from plants but in many instances the quality of the seedlings will be inferior to that of the parents. This will certainly be the case if parents are F_1 or F_2 hybrids, which have been selected and crossed to give a generation of plants of desirable and uniform characteristics. It is generally best to start with fresh seed from a reliable source. A packet of seeds will normally produce many more plants than you will need for one season in a container garden but seed in an open packet does not always last well until the following year. If you have friends who enjoy gardening, it may be worth sharing seeds or young plants so that you all have a wider range of mature plants and some spares in reserve in case of a failure.

The equipment you need for raising seeds indoors is very simple, consisting of starting medium, either loam-based or soil-less, and clean seed trays or pots, which must have drainage holes. Cleanliness is important for good results and

an advantage of plastic containers is that they are easily scrubbed.

Place a layer of clean crocks (pieces of broken clay pots) in the bottom of pots. Fill the trays or pots with medium and shake it down. Soil-less media should be pressed down lightly with the fingers. Soil-based mixes need to be consolidated more firmly and the most effective way is to use a block of wood. Once firmed, the surface of the medium should be about 1.25cm (½in) below the rim. Before sowing make sure that the medium is thoroughly moistened, either by standing trays or pots in a basin of water or by watering with a fine rose, and then allow the containers to drain.

Seed size varies greatly from plant to plant but whatever the size you should aim to plant evenly and thinly to give seedlings a good chance and to make subsequent handling easier. Large seeds, such as those of nasturtiums (*Tropaeolum majus*), are easily spaced out and pressed into the medium. Finer seed can be sown directly from the packet but it is often easier to take a pinch between finger and thumb and sprinkle over the surface of the medium. Dust-like seed is best mixed with a medium, such as fine dry sand, to make it easier to scatter evenly. Once they have been sown, lightly cover seeds except the finest with a layer of the potting mix.

For many seeds germination is more consistent if light is excluded. This can be done by placing a cover over the tray or pot. However, a close watch needs to be kept so that the cover is removed as soon as the seedlings start to emerge. Keep trays or pots at an even temperature, ideally about 18°C (64°F), and make sure that the planting medium does not dry out.

Germination of many annuals takes between one and three weeks. Once the seedlings have emerged, place the containers in a well-lit position. The risk of seedlings collapsing as a result of fungal attack (damping-off) can be minimized by watering them with a fungicide.

Seedlings should be transplanted to trays filled with a richer growing medium once the seed leaves are fully developed. It is important to handle

seedlings as little as possible. Gently lift out a clump with the point of a knife or a small dibber. Take seedlings individually, holding by a single leaf, and drop into a hole made with a dibber, spacing plants at a distance of about 5cm (2in). When a tray is planted up, remember to water thoroughly with a fine rose.

Keep plants at the temperature at which they were germinated until they are making good growth and only then begin to accustom them to lower temperatures. This is the procedure known as "hardening off". The ideal place for hardening off plants is a cold frame, which is like a glazed box which will protect plants if there is frost but in which the ventilation can be gradually increased until the light or lid is completely removed. For the first few days open the frame only slightly during the day, then gradually build up the ventilation until the frame is completely open. Once plants have been thoroughly hardened off they are then ready to be planted out in whatever containers you have planned for them.

If you have no frame, you may have to move containers outdoors when the weather is mild and bring them inside at night. Placing plants at the base of a wall or hedge gives them some protection from strong winds and driving rain, and they can be covered, for example with newspaper, if there is a risk of night frost.

Biennials and perennials can be sown outdoors in early summer. The seed bed should be well prepared in advance, dug over in autumn and then the surface broken down to a fine tilth before planting. Unless the weather has been very dry it is generally not necessary to water the bed before sowing. The seeds are sown in a drill, a shallow furrow, the depth of which depends on the size of the seed being sown. Sow thinly and then cover the seeds lightly by raking over the top of the drill and firming. The seedlings need to be watered regularly in dry weather and kept free of weeds. Once seedlings are growing strongly they can be transplanted to a nursery bed, where they are grown on until lifted and planted in containers in the autumn.

Above, left: Shoots chosen for cuttings should be young and healthy. Here a cutting is being taken from a pelargonium in late summer. A sharp knife or razor blade is used to make a clean cut just below a joint before the cutting is inserted in a pot filled with a free-draining medium low in nutrients, such as a seed medium.

Above, right: A tray of pelargonium cuttings, each in an individual pot, is being thoroughly watered before being placed in a close moist atmosphere to encourage rooting. Pelargoniums, which are not hardy and therefore need to be overwintered in frost-free conditions, take extremely easily from cuttings. Old plants can be discarded annually.

TAKING CUTTINGS

The ease with which many plants can be increased by vegetative means, for example from cuttings, makes it possible to raise duplicates of particularly desirable plants. For the container gardener these vegetative methods of propagation, especially from stem cuttings, are useful ways of maintaining stocks of half-hardy or tender plants (whether herbaceous perennials or shrubs) that are unlikely to survive outdoors in winter. Cuttings can be taken during the growing season and overwintered in a frost-free place.

Take cuttings 5-10cm (2-4in) long of non-flowering shoots from healthy vigorous plants, making sure they do not carry pests. Softwood cuttings are taken in the first half of summer and semi-hardwood cuttings in the second half.

Cut each cutting across the base with a razor blade or sharp knife just below a joint and cut off the bottom two pairs of leaves. Cuttings can be dipped in a hormone rooting powder before being inserted in pots containing a loam-based seed medium or other medium low in nutrients. Softwood and semi-hardwood cuttings need to be kept warm and moist until they strike but they should not be placed in direct sunlight.

You can improvise good propagating conditions simply by placing a clear plastic bag over the pot and cuttings and keeping in a warm place, such as a kitchen. If you are going to do a lot of propagating it might be worth buying a propagator that incorporates some method of bottom heat.

Softwood cuttings will generally root in two to three weeks and semi-hardwood cuttings in about a month. Once they have rooted, remove cuttings from their close environment and pot each one of them individually, using a good all-purpose potting medium.

Hardwood cuttings, which are taken in autumn or early winter, are useful for propagating hardy shrubs and will generally strike satisfactorily if set in a trench in the open garden.

PLANTING

Your aim should be to get plants into their new container with a minimum of disturbance and delay. Make sure, therefore, that all the equipment you need is ready and that you have thought through how you want your container to look once plants have reached maturity.

Provided that you are vigilant about watering and feed regularly, it is possible to plant closely to create a full effect quickly. For example, annuals that in the open garden might be spaced 15-20cm (6-8in) apart might be planted only 7.5cm (3in) apart in containers. Many shrubs, especially those that tolerate dry conditions such as most of the cotoneasters, can be closely underplanted. Maples (*Acer*), camellias and rhododendrons, however, like a moist medium and should not be crowded by other plants. They generally do best planted on their own.

Have containers filled with potting mix (if they are heavy, place them in their final position before filling) and water plants in their original containers and leave to drain. When they have drained, plant in sequence, with large central or background plants first and smaller plants for the foreground and sides later. To remove a plant from its original container, invert the pot and place the fingers of one hand either side of the plant's stem and over the surface of the soil. Tap the pot lightly and pull it away from the root ball with the other hand. Unless the plant is root bound, it is better not to loosen the roots; using a trowel, dig out a hole in the soil large enough to take the root ball so that the plant will sit at the same level as it did in its original container.

There are a few exceptions to this, such as clematis, which should be planted slightly deeper than they were originally but, if in any doubt, follow the general rule. Except in the case of trailers, which it is often best to start with a slight lean outwards, check that the plant is standing vertically before firming the potting mix round the root ball. Soil-based media are best well firmed but do not compact soil-less media. Once the container is planted, water thoroughly.

In general, if bulbs are to be combined with other plants it is best to leave their planting until last but in the case of tulips, for example, you then need a narrow trowel to take out soil so that the bulb can be dropped in to a depth of about 15cm (6in). A spectacular massed effect can be achieved with bulbs by planting them in a tub or large pot in two horizontal layers, making sure that the bulbs do not touch.

WATERING

It is difficult to overstate the extent to which container-grown plants are dependent on the gardener for their supplies of water. Their roots, unlike those of plants in the open garden, cannot search out moisture; they must wait for what is provided. Rain is sometimes little help. Buildings can cast rain shadow so that window boxes and other containers close to walls or fences are barely dampened, even in heavy downpours. Equally, in an open position the foliage of plants can be so dense that most rainwater is shed by the leaves and does not get through to the soil.

The frequency with which plants need watering depends on several factors, among them the nature of the growing medium, the amount of leafy growth, temperature, rainfall, exposure to direct sunshine and also exposure to wind. Just as there is a danger of plants suffering from lack of water, there is a risk of them being overwatered, especially when containers do not have adequate drainage holes or a layer of rough material such as crocks in the bottom. The best course is to give the medium in containers a really thorough soaking, watering until water comes out of the drainage holes, repeating again when the medium is almost dry – you can use a finger to feel it just below the surface.

It is generally best to water in early morning or evening and you should make sure that the water gets to the soil and is not shed by leaves. If watering in bright sunny weather, avoid getting water on leaves, for otherwise they are likely to scorch. You need to be particularly vigilant in summer, checking containers regularly in the morning and evening. Even in spring and autumn containers can dry out quickly if there is a combination of bright sunshine and strong wind.

Although tap water will do for most plants there are some areas where the supply is markedly alkaline and this does not suit lime-haters such as rhododendrons and camellias. For these plants it may be necessary to gather rain water.

With a watering can or standard hose it may be difficult to get water to hanging baskets or wall-mounted troughs without using a set of steps. It is possible, however, to fit rigid extensions to hoses that can direct a flow of water above head height and there are also simple pumps that are useful, provided there are not too many containers to be watered. If you have had experience of watering an awkwardly placed hanging basket you may well think it worth having a pulley system or a rise-and-fall fixture that makes it possible to lower a basket for watering and general maintenance.

It is often in the summer, when container-grown plants need most attention, that gardeners are away for holidays or breaks. Always water thoroughly before going away and, if at all possible, stand containers in a lightly shaded and sheltered position. If a reliable neighbor cannot be persuaded to come in to look after your plants, the proprietary reservoirs that can be incorporated in window boxes and large containers will certainly help for a few days but they need to be put in position at planting time.

You can rig up your own reservoir and drip feed by running strips of capillary matting from a raised tank or basin to containers placed at a lower level. Smaller containers, which dry out more quickly, are more easily managed for they can be placed in a tray on a layer of capillary matting, part of which lies in a reservoir well filled with water. The water works its way from the reservoir to the tray and up into the pot.

The amateur using containers on a large scale might find it worth considering some of the adaptations of automated systems that have been developed for nurseries. There is a capillary system in which the pots are stood on a tray of aggregate which is fed an automated supply of water. A system allowing a freer arrangement of containers feeds a trickle of water to individual containers through fine tubes running from a main pipe. Various sprinkling systems are also possible but these are generally of limited use with container plants for, setting aside other disadvantages, such as possible leaf and flower damage, there is a good chance that the water will not be sufficiently directed to get to the growing medium.

Although your aim should be to water plants before they wilt, there may be occasional lapses when pots dry out. Act quickly when you see signs of stress, for most plants soon reach a stage when they cannot be revived or, if they can, it will only be as poor specimens that never live up to their original potential. If at all possible, plunge the whole pot in a bucket of water so that the rim is just below the surface and leave until the soil is thoroughly saturated.

FEEDING AND REPOTTING

Even when you start your plants in a good medium containing a well-balanced supply of nutrients, it is worth maintaining a feeding program during the growing season. It is not just that plants use up nutrients; some are washed out by regular watering and need to be replaced. Additional feeding is especially important when you are using soil-less media, for in these the nutrients are exhausted relatively quickly.

Fertilizers that are released slowly over a long period are available in the form of sticks and pellets. But there are also quicker-acting fertilizers that are generally applied in liquid form, watered into the medium. For an even faster response from plants a liquid feed can be sprayed on to leaves. This should never be done in bright sunshine but instead in the evening or on a dull day. Whatever fertilizer is used, it should be applied at the strengths and frequencies recommended by the manufacturers.

Shrubs in large containers and perennials may need to be repotted from time to time. After a few years perennials tend to become woody at the center and when this happens they should be lifted in the dormant season and divided, the old growth being discarded and only the newer growth on the outer edge of the plant being reused in fresh potting medium.

In the case of shrubs check the state of the soil and root system every year in the dormant season by scraping away the top layer of soil. If it is obvious that the roots have formed a tight mass almost filling the container, repot the plant in a slightly larger container. Use fresh potting mix containing a slow-release fertilizer and, if necessary, lightly prune the roots. Shrubs that do not need repotting should be given a dressing of slow-release fertilizer every spring. Scrape away the top 5cm (2in) or so of medium and replace with a fresh mixture into which has been incorporated bonemeal or a balanced all-purpose fertilizer.

DEADHEADING, PRUNING AND TRAINING

Many ornamentals that are grown in containers need very little management beyond the removal of dead leaves and the tidying up of straggling growth. With most flowering plants, however, it is worth taking trouble to deadhead regularly. It is not just that plants look rejuvenated when faded flowers are removed. Most of those that flower prolifically in summer will give a longer and better display if frequently deadheaded. Energy that would otherwise go into producing more flowers or making vigorous growth is diverted when plants are allowed to set seed.

Most shrubs suitable for growing in containers need little pruning other than the removal of damaged, diseased or dead wood. The Japanese maples (*Acer palmatum*), for instance, should not have their beautifully intricate branches thinned or shortened or else the character of the plants is lost. Flowering evergreens such as camellias and rhododendrons should be deadheaded and the little trimming that may be required can be done in mid- to late spring. To prevent them becoming straggly, trim lavenders (*Lavandula*) and heaths (*Erica*) in mid-spring but avoid shearing them down to an unnaturally flat top. Box (*Buxus*) and other evergreens that are used for topiary can be trimmed about every six weeks throughout the summer if a sharply defined shape is required but for most people one trim in late summer is generally sufficient.

Some deciduous flowering shrubs and climbers flower on wood that is one year old. This is true of *Clematis alpina* and *C. macropetala*. Any pruning of these plants is best done immediately after flowering. Other shrubs and climbers, including fuchsias and *Clematis viticella*, produce flowers on the current season's growth and these plants are best pruned in spring. Hardy fuchsias, for example, can be cut back almost to soil level. This method of pruning is often employed on mophead hydrangeas but these do better if only a proportion of old growth is cut out each spring. Miniature and patio roses should have all weak growth cut out entirely and main stems and strong laterals shortened by about a third.

If in doubt about pruning the best course is to limit drastic cutting to the removal of dead, diseased and damaged wood and to trim lightly after flowering.

Where supports are necessary, for example with a standard fuchsia or a climber to be trained up a wall, the support, generally as inconspicuous as possible, should be put in position at planting time and the plants tied in as they make growth. However, the support itself can be made into an attractive feature, as is shown by the spiral on pages 82-3.

PLANT TROUBLES

There is no complete defense against pests and diseases but many problems can be avoided by taking simple common-sense measures. The first thing is to start with healthy plants and to grow them in pots that have been thoroughly cleaned and preferably sterilized, before being filled with fresh growing mix. By growing plants in the conditions that suit them and feeding them regularly they will normally make vigorous growth.

When, despite the measures you have taken, plants succumb to pests and diseases, you may have to be more ruthless than the gardener who is working on a grander scale, for in the intimacy of the contained garden blemishes are all too obvious. If it is impossible to identify the problem and treat promptly an ailing short-lived plant such as an annual or biennial, by far the most sensible course is to get rid of it, preferably burning it and, if this is not possible, disposing of it with the household rubbish.

Below : A wigwam of bamboo canes is an easy climbing frame for fast-growing annuals such as *Ipomoea tricolor* or beans, and twiggy branches are a good support for dwarf peas and sweet peas.

Measures can be taken to control a number of pests and diseases that are fairly readily identifiable. Some of the larger pests, such as snails, slugs, caterpillars and earwigs, are easily spotted, especially if plants are examined by flashlight at night. Pick them off by hand and destroy them.

Sap-sucking pests such as aphids (greenfly and blackfly) and whitefly cause distorted and stunted growth and can spread serious viral diseases. They can be controlled by a variety of sprays, including some based on pyrethrum.

Fungal diseases affect a number of plants, some roses, for example, being particularly susceptible to mildew and black spot. Infections can be controlled by spraying with fungicides, such as formulations containing benomyl. Much more difficult to treat are the rots resulting from bacterial infection. Plants suffering from these or viral infection, which cause stunted growth and mottling of flowers and foliage, should be destroyed to protect uninfected plants.

When there has been a problem with disease, dispose of soil in which infected plants have been growing and be particular about sterilizing containers before reusing them.

WINTER PRECAUTIONS

To keep half-hardy and tender plants going through winter you need to bring them under cover and keep them in a frost-free greenhouse or conservatory. You can risk leaving plants of borderline hardiness, such as hebes, outdoors but it is worth taking cuttings so that if the parent plant is lost there will be young plants to take its place.

Plants of borderline hardiness left outdoors can be given some protection. Plunging the pot up to its rim in the earth in a sheltered part of a garden will help protect the roots from severe frosts. If the container cannot be plunged in the garden, wrap it in straw held in by burlap. The part of the plant above ground should also be protected by straw or dry bracken held inside a frame of netting or burlap firmly supported by canes. Straw and burlap can also be wrapped around vulnerable pots to protect them from frost.

HANGING BASKETS

There is something miraculous in an eye-catching hanging basket brimming with summer flowers. Such a *tour de force* of color and greenery does not seem entirely the work of the gardener's hands. Perhaps this is at the root of the snobbery that sees the hanging basket as the comic turn of gardening. More sensible than this patronizing approach is to recognize that hanging baskets have much in common with flower arrangements. A successful hanging basket, like a successful arrangement, is positioned to hold the eye by a skillful blending of flowers and foliage, all brought together in a very limited compass. Unlike most flower arrangements, however, a hanging basket gives pleasure for months on end.

What surprises everyone who has successfully planted a hanging basket is the way living plants arrange themselves. There are, of course, a few basics that cannot be neglected. You need to start with a reasonable selection of plants that will develop into a well-balanced combination of colors. Watering and feeding must be kept up and to keep the basket smart you need to trim off dead flowers and leaves regularly and occasionally cut off over-vigorous growths. But, virtually unaided, plants interweave with a nonchalant artistry that gives the hanging basket its special appeal.

The lavish repetition of this exuberant summer planting, dominated by colorful fuchsias, pelargoniums, lobelias and petunias, succeeds in creating an opulent rather than a subtle effect but these hanging baskets do brighten what could be a rather somber exterior.

33

Below : Baskets should not be placed where they may bang heads or impede use of a doorway. This splendid pair planted with lobelias and busy lizzies (*Impatiens*) flank a seldom-used entrance.

POSITIONING HANGING BASKETS

A well-watered hanging basket filled with soil and plants can be a very heavy object. It is too late to be looking about for a place to hang it when it has already been planted up. In some instances it may be possible to attach baskets to existing beams or overhead ironwork, which must be strong and sound. If the basket is to be suspended from a bracket or attached directly to a wall, the bracket or basket should be screwed into drilled holes, which in brick walls need to be filled with wall plugs. As a general rule, avoid fastening wall baskets directly against house walls as there can be a risk of damp penetration. A swivel connection between the chains of the basket and the support is very useful, simplifying maintenance and allowing all sides to be turned to the light.

The position of a basket must also allow for easy watering. At any height above eye level you will need steps to get to it.

. Finding the right position to please the eye will depend very much on the layout of your home. A single basket might make a captivating focal point at the end of a path or cheer the view from a window. You may prefer to plant hanging baskets in groups: as a row along a veranda, allowing, say, at least 30cm (12in) between baskets, as a cluster hung at different heights from the solid beam of a pergola, or as a matching pair flanking a doorway. Whatever your intention, make sure that you experiment with the empty basket before planting it up so that you are happy about the position.

ESSENTIAL MATERIALS

As the step-by-step sequences (pages 36-7, 40-1 and 42-3) show, a wide range of materials can be used to create an effective hanging basket. Most conventional kinds are based on a fairly open frame that can be lined to hold in a lightweight potting mix that will provide the anchor and nutrients for plants (for a summary of media see page 24). An open framework allows plants to be inserted at various levels in the basket so that their mature growth eventually conceals the frame. Most commercially made frames are of plastic-

Below, left: Baskets can be mounted on strong wall brackets firmly fixed on exterior house or garden walls. This planting includes petunias, lobelias and fuchsias.

Below, right : If hanging a basket from a beam, check that it can be watered easily, adjusting the supports if necessary. This planting includes pelargoniums and monkey flowers (*Mimulus*).

coated wire, with diameters ranging from about 25cm (10in) to 50cm (20in). Other frames of the same basic construction have one flat side and are for attaching to walls. The largest of these are in the shape of hay racks.

Several different materials are used as lining. In choosing your liner you should bear in mind that environmentalists have warned against the collection of sphagnum from the wild and the excessive exploitation of peat reserves. Many gardeners still favor sphagnum moss, for even when plants are just getting established the basket looks green and natural from below. Others find plastic perfectly satisfactory and they argue that a dark color is hardly noticeable once plants begin to make growth. The plastic is easily slit with a sharp knife to allow plants to be inserted at different levels. Commercially manufactured liners include rigid peat-based basins. One of an appropriate size is dropped into the frame and it can be cut wherever you want to insert plants. Another commercial kind consists of a circular sheet of synthetic material cut in such a way that when the sheet is put into a frame the segments overlap so that the sheet fits the shape.

PLANTING A SUMMER BASKET

You will need :
Plastic-coated wire-frame basket, about 35cm
   (14in) in diameter
340g (12oz) sphagnum moss
Circle of black plastic sheeting, about 60cm
   (24in) in diameter
5 liters (1 gallon) soil-less potting medium
Scissors
Trowel
Metal chain
Sturdy metal hook

3-4 trailing lobelias
3 *Campanula garganica*
3 *Felicia amelloides* 'Variegata'
3 white verbenas
2 *Fuchsia* 'Tom Thumb'
2 pink ivy-leaved pelargoniums
1 dark red regal pelargonium
1 *Tradescantia pendula*

For a long summer display a hanging basket is best
planted up in mid- to late spring. Remember,
however, to harden the plants off before hanging
it outdoors. This basket looks delightful here but
for the best results it should be permanently sited
in a less shady position.
1 Assemble all the necessary materials.
2 Line the basket with moss up to about half way
and lay a circle of plastic as an inner lining over
this. Cut a short slit in the base of the plastic for
drainage. Add some potting mix and plant three
or four trailing plants such as lobelias so that they
are worked through the frame at the height of
the plastic lining. The procedure is essentially the
same when liners other than sphagnum are used.
Make short cross slits for plants in the top half of
full plastic or peat-based liners.
3 Continue lining the basket with sphagnum. At
fairly even spaces work more plants through the
frame and add potting mix.
4 Complete lining the basket with sphagnum and
finish planting from the top, filling with potting
mix to just below the rim. Stand the basket on
the top of a bucket and water thoroughly.

SUMMER SETPIECE

The classic hanging basket is a summer setpiece and the key to its success is brimming vitality controlled by a harmonious color sense. There is no shortage of plants to choose from among hardy and half-hardy annuals or hardy and tender perennials.

A few bushy plants are useful to give a slightly domed effect. Calceolarias, busy lizzies (*Impatiens*), zonal pelargoniums, pansies and the similar but smaller-flowered violas as well as short-growing fuchsias, such as the red and purple 'Tom Thumb', are all suitable, tending to sprawl rather than make leggy growth. Some spectacular foliage plants that are often grown under glass also make excellent centerpieces. The color range in *Coleus blumei,* often combined in a single frilled or attractively lobed leaf, extends from pale yellow, through pinks and reds, to maroon and deepest purple. To shape the plant pinch out the growing tips. Another plant with striking foliage is *Begonia rex.* The large asymmetrical leaves are in metallic silver, pinks, reds and purples, often combined in arresting patterns.

What counts for more than the bushy plants when it comes to creating a miniature garden in the sky are the trailers. Many good flowering plants trail naturally or have trailing or pendulous forms. These include fibrous-rooted and tuberous begonias, black-eyed susan vine (*Thunbergia alata*), *Campanula isophylla*, creeping jenny (*Lysimachia nummularia*), fuchsias, lobelias, nasturtiums, ivy-leaved pelargoniums, petunias and verbenas.

Some of these, such as nasturtiums and ivy-leaved pelargoniums, have attractive foliage that sets flowers off well. In many combinations, however, you will need trailing foliage plants. Ivies, variegated or in shades of green, are invaluable, as are the various forms of *Helichrysum petiolatum.* Many good trailers are variegated, including the dead nettle *Lamium maculatum.* 'White Nancy' is a particularly lovely cultivar and a longer trailer is the variegated ground ivy (*Nepeta hederacea* 'Variegata'), the variegation showing up the pretty edge of the leaves.

There are also several trailers to borrow from among houseplants. *Tradescantia fluminensis* 'Quicksilver' has an almost pure-white striped variegation while the striping in *T. pendula* is of silver against purple and green. In bright green one of the best house plants available is asparagus fern, *A. setaceus*.

VARIATIONS ON HANGING CONTAINERS

There are many commercially made containers in terracotta and plastic that are designed to be suspended in the same way as hanging baskets. However, like most improvised containers, these do not have an open framework and all the planting must be at the top.

Two examples of improvisation are shown in the step-by-step sequences that follow. The best of the improvised or specially manufactured containers are ornamental in their own right, as I think our table basket and colander are. The worst, however, can look simply incongruous swinging above the ground. A conventional basket might look very much better.

Opposite: Summer favorites mainly in the magenta, blue and mauve color range include lobelias, fuchsias and petunias, and make a full and long-lasting display.

Left, top : Lobelias and the foliage plant *Helichrysum petiolatum* have made a wonderfully brimming summer basket to which fuchsias will soon add their rich tones.

Left, bottom : The creamy green foliage of *Helichrysum petiolatum* 'Limelight' makes it an easy companion and a useful link between difficult colors. Here it is planted with lobelias, nasturtiums and petunias.

PLANTING AN UNUSUAL BASKET

You will need :
Ornamental wire basket, about 22cm (9in)
    square and 13cm (5in) deep
340g (12oz) sphagnum moss
50cm (20in) square sheet of black plastic
3 liters (0.7 gallon) soil-less potting medium
Scissors
Trowel

At least 6 pansies
3 variegated ivy plants (*Hedera helix* cultivars)

Ornamental wire baskets that are normally used for table decoration are easily adapted as hanging baskets. Unlike conventional hanging baskets, they are attractive in themselves and suit a light kind of planting.

Other kinds of basket could also be used. Wicker is a visually attractive choice but as a material it does not have a long life and a wicker container will have to be replaced regularly. For any unusual container the most important requirement is that it has good drainage.

In the sequence shown here, pansies are mixed with variegated ivies. Such simple and restrained planting can be used to show off any pretty container, especially in the off-season from early spring to early summer, when the ideal plants are early-flowering pansies.

1 Assemble the materials needed for planting the basket.
2 Line the basket with moss to just below the top edge. This lining is not essential but greatly improves the appearance of a lightly planted basket.
3 Lay the plastic liner in the basket and cut one or two short slits in the base for drainage. Add a little potting mix and then begin planting, working potting mix round the plants and then topping up to just below the edge of the inner liner. With a larger basket of this kind it would be worth inserting some plants from the side, slitting the plastic liner where necessary. Water the basket well before hanging.

USING A COLANDER

You will need :
Enamel colander, about 27cm (10in) in
    diameter
Circle of black plastic sheeting, about 49cm
    (19in) in diameter
3 liters (0.7 gallon) soil-less potting medium
Scissors
Trowel
Strong nylon string
Butcher's hook

6-8 nasturtiums (a mixture of *Tropaeolum majus*
    and *T. peregrinum*), grown from seed in seed-
    starting mix.
3-4 curled parsley plants, purchased

Colanders are among many containers that can be
adapted as hanging baskets. The large ones are of
a convenient size, all have the necessary drainage
holes and it is easy to attach supporting wires.
    The color of the colander influenced the
choice of the trailing plants. Climbing nasturtiums
are too vigorous for a container of this size. The
curled parsley is an unusual but complementary
foliage plant. Charming as it is, this is not an ideal
position for such a planting; it needs more sun to
thrive.
1 Plan your hanging basket well in advance. The
liner can be, as here, one of those available
commercially or simply a piece of plastic sheeting
with short slits cut at the base for drainage.
2 Sow seed in pots of seed-starting mix,
preferably under glass in early to mid-spring.
Later sowings can be left outdoors. Parsley
germinates erratically and it is probably easier to
start with young plants.
3 Plants raised under glass must be hardened off,
either individually or in the container once it is
planted up. Lay the liner in the container and
partially fill it with potting medium.
4 All planting in a colander must be from the top.
Space plants around the edge and in the center;
this planting is very close for a full effect. Fill in
with potting mix to just below the edge of the
liner. Water thoroughly.

BROADENING THE PLANT RANGE

Although hanging baskets are generally planted as mixtures of fairly familiar flowers and foliage, there is scope for trying out less commonly used plants. It is worth adding to the foliage plants already recommended on page 17. The ubiquitous spider plant (*Chlorophytum comosum* 'Variegatum') has arching cream and green leaves and dangles young plantlets engagingly. Baby's tears (*Soleirolia soleirolii*), a creeping plant for sun or shade which has tiny bright green leaves (there are also golden and variegated forms), will spread around the base of a basket. An easy trailer is *Plectranthus fruticosus* and *P. oertendahlii* is a sprawling plant with green veins on bronze-green and almost circular leaves.

The light arching fronds of ferns are a lovely addition to baskets hung in shadier positions. In summer the range can be extended to include ferns that are not fully hardy, such as the maidenhair fern (*Adiantum capillus-veneris*) and *Pteris argyraea*.

Hardy herbaceous perennials are not much used in hanging baskets and yet some, especially those with good foliage, are just as valuable in containers as they are in the open garden. A variety of the common bugle (*Ajuga reptans*), 'Burgundy Glow' has foliage with cream variegation and a flushing of deep red. It sprawls and makes a useful short trailer. More startling is the vivid variegation in red, cream and green of *Houttuynia cordata* 'Chameleon'. One of the best greens is that found in lady's mantle (*Alchemilla mollis*), with soft fan-shaped leaves and sprays of tiny lime-green, star-shaped flowers. The leaves of *Fragaria* 'Pink Panda' are a brighter green and there is a long succession of small pink flowers. *Heuchera* 'Palace Purple' has glossy dark purple leaves which are a handsome foil for pinks and reds, even yellows. Better suited to accompany yellows, however, are the gold-mottled leaves of *Tolmiea menziesii* 'Taff's Gold'.

Among useful plants there are a few herbs that go well with ornamentals. The best of these are chives, parsley and variegated mints, with the

dense rich green leaves of parsley going particularly well with yellow flowers such as nasturtiums
(*Tropaeolum majus*).

EXTENDING THE SEASON

In warm climates, the difficulty of achieving a rich
and vigorous planting between autumn and spring
explains the generally neglected state of hanging
baskets for half the year. There are a few simple
ways of filling the gap, however. Although the
freest-flowering plants in the off-season are bulbs,
their upright growth unfortunately does not make
them ideally suited to life in hanging baskets. Early-
flowering pansies are the most reliable standby
and a good ivy makes a suitable companion. For a
more lavish planting experiment with polyanthus
and other early primrose hybrids.

Many gardeners find that it is easier to extend
the main season rather than plant for the off-
season. In an Indian summer late-planted baskets
can make a magnificent display, fuchsias often
doing exceptionally well. The season can be
extended at the other end by early planting of
baskets with hardy material such as pansies and
Tropaeolum majus hybrids. If you have a greenhouse, glassed-in porch or other protected area
you can even start a basket off early with half-
hardy plants, ready to go outside when the
weather is warm enough.

Opposite : The hardy perennial *Tolmiea
menziesii* 'Taff's Gold' makes an ideal companion
for the yellow-flowered *Tagetes erecta,
Argyranthemum frutescens* 'Jamaica Primrose' and
Lantana camara.
Right, top : Creeping jenny (*Lysimachia
nummularia*) is an easy evergreen perennial with
yellow flowers. It is planted alone, as is another
good perennial, *Heuchera* 'Palace Purple', seen in
the background.
Right, bottom : The delicate patterns and
graceful arching fronds of ferns are shown off to
good effect in hanging baskets and the added
advantage of these plants is that they do well in
shady positions.

PLANTING A BRACKET BASKET

You will need :
Bracket basket, about 90cm (35in) long,
   25cm (10in) wide and 17cm (7in) deep
2 buckets of straw
Black plastic netting or sheeting, about 140cm
   (55in) long and 60cm (23in) wide
15 liters (3 gallons) soil-based potting medium
Scissors
Trowel
6cm (2½in) screws and corresponding wall
   plugs (if necessary)

12-15 plants, including :
Acaena 'Pewter' (New Zealand burr), apple mint,
   bergenias, curry plant, euonymus, *Euphorbia
   myrsinites*, *Helichrysum angustifolium*, *Heuchera*
   'Palace Purple' and hosta

The model for large bracket baskets like that
shown opposite planted with a mixture of hardy
perennials and low-growing shrubs is the stable
hay rack. This example is made of heavy-gauge
plastic-covered wire. The plants have been
selected for quality of foliage, giving a range of
color, leaf size and texture.

1 Decide where you are going to attach your
basket and assemble your materials. Attach the
basket firmly using screws (wall plugs are
necessary if screws are going into brickwork).
2 Line the basket with straw. This is not an
essential step but straw forms a natural-looking
base in keeping with the hay-rack theme. In a
smaller bracket basket moss could be used but
plastic alone is environmentally preferable.
3 Lay the inner liner over the straw. Black plastic
sheeting is a more readily available alternative. If
using plastic cut three or four short slits in the
base for drainage. A few slits are even advisable in
the netting. Put in a first layer of potting mix.
4 As plants are placed in position, fill with potting
mix to just below the level of the inner liner.
Trailers can also be inserted in the side by slitting
the liner. When planting is completed water
thoroughly.

WINDOW BOXES

Often the window box is, quite simply, the only practical solution for those who live in apartments and do not have a garden, terrace or balcony to transform into a little paradise. Skilled plantsmen whose window boxes are a distillation of great garden wisdom and novices making their first experiments in growing plants all agree that it is a particularly pleasurable kind of gardening. What it lacks in scale it makes up for in intimacy, with cherished plants lovingly tended and frequently scrutinized.

Although this is gardening on a very reduced scale, an amazingly wide range of plants can be grown. The typical ingredients of a window box are spring bulbs followed by cheerful summer flowers, especially hardy and half-hardy annuals. But many other plants can be grown successfully, including small shrubs, rock-garden plants and herbs. There is a more theatrical side to window-box gardening that often appeals to those with a whole house to deck with flowers. The most ambitious co-ordinated schemes can be Babylonian in scale. Even when less extreme, with flowers spilling from a single cottage window, the window box plays an important role in dressing the house.

In vertical gardening on an impressive scale window boxes of ivy-leaved pelargoniums make vivid accents on a wall clothed in *Parthenocissus tricuspidata* (virginia creeper). On the upper floor the boxes are fitted below the window sill so that light can still get in.

49

Opposite: Following a color theme through a variety of containers, with taller plants at ground level, can work well. Planting includes sweet peas (*Lathyrus*), hollyhocks (*Alcea*) and *Cosmos*.

Below : A window box above a door needs a drip tray and will have to be watered from steps. This box, planted with daffodils, hyacinths and ivy, enhances a handsome but severe frontage.

WHICH WINDOWS FOR BOXES?

Window-box gardeners can be divided very roughly into two broad categories. The first, and it is a group for whom I have very warm feelings, comprises those who look out of their windows at their cherished collections of plants. Generally speaking, they are apartment dwellers who, although gardenless, have set their hearts on growing garden plants. They are lucky if they have a choice of sill and it is rarely more than between one that is sunny and another that is shady.

The other broad category is made up of the house decorators. They view, and invite you to view, their window boxes from outside rather than from inside their homes. They have choice about where they are going to put their window boxes but, given half a chance, use all available sills to create a wonderful cascading vertical garden.

For both categories there are practical points to take into account. Many windows open outwards and where this is the case window boxes sitting on sills will be in the way. The best solution is to have metal brackets fitted below the window so that when a window box is supported by them the top growth comes more or less level with the sill. Brackets, which should be screwed into wall plugs in walls made of brick or mortar, must be capable of carrying the considerable weight of container, moist soil and plants. It is advisable to have them fitted by a professional.

Even where there are sash windows there are advantages in having window boxes supported at a level below the sill. When boxes sit right against windows rain can sometimes splash soil against the glass, especially in winter before a planting of bulbs comes through. If the windows are small, as in many cottages, even a box of low plants can block out valuable light.

Reasonable access for watering is another point to bear in mind. While most ground-floor window boxes are easily watered from outside, those on upper floors will need to be watered from inside the house. To water an awkwardly placed box, for instance one above a door, a pump-operated spray may be the easiest solution.

CHOOSING BOXES

Traditional window boxes are made of wood or terracotta and to many people these are still the most attractive materials. Terracotta needs no treatment at all and, provided the window box is frost resistant, will last for years. Wood does not have an indefinite life but a well-made wooden window box that is treated with a preservative (one that is not harmful to plants) will last for many years. The construction of a simple wooden window box would defeat me but many others would not find it difficult.

Window boxes are also made of other materials, including concrete, fiberglass and plastic. Sills that are not strong enough to take the weight of heavy window boxes, such as those made of terracotta or concrete, should not be carrying window boxes at all. Concrete weathers surprisingly well but fiberglass and plastic often remain shiningly conspicuous, although they will generally be hidden by vigorous plant growth in summer.

For window boxes that are to have seasonal changes of planting it is useful to have lightweight liners, generally of plastic, which can be custom built or improvised. All liners must have drainage holes. When bulbs have finished flowering, for example, they can be taken out in their liner, which can be replaced with another liner already planted up with summer flowers.

A properly made window box, furnished with several drainage holes, is generally about 15-20cm (6-8in) deep and wide and, unless custom built, in lengths up to about 120cm (4ft). Check your window sills carefully before buying boxes.

Ideally these should make a fairly close fit but even so should be firmly secured where there is any risk of them being dislodged. Wooden boxes are relatively easy to fix to frames but others may need to be held in by wedges or by a restraining bar, wire or even a heavy-duty nylon thread fixed to the frame.

Ensure that window boxes are raised slightly on small blocks so that water can drain away easily. If you use a drip tray (advisable for window boxes on upper floors), the blocks should sit in the tray.

Opposite : A small terracotta window box makes a lovely container for a pink, white and blue combination of zonal pelargoniums, petunias and lobelias. Terracotta remains for many people the ideal material for a container, although once it has weathered concrete, too, can look very attractive. This combination of plants and container could be used at a ground-floor window but would not be stable enough for upper floors. If there is any risk of instability, make sure window boxes are firmly secured.

Above : Where windows open outwards, boxes cannot be set directly on sills without being in the way. This combination of lobelias, pelargoniums and fuchsias rests on the sill of a sash window, but even houseowners with such windows often prefer to mount boxes on brackets just below window-sill level to allow more light into the room and to avoid the problem of splashing. Wall brackets can also be used to support troughs and boxes in other positions on walls. Grouped as here, they can soften an austere exterior.

PLANTING A SUMMER WINDOW BOX

You will need :

Wooden window box, about 90cm (35in) long, 23cm (9in) wide and 18cm (7in deep)
Rigid plastic liner with drainage holes to fit window box
5 large handfuls of crocks or expanded clay granules
10 liters (2 gallons) soil-less potting medium
Trowel

3 osteospermums
3 red verbenas
2-3 petunias
2 dwarf tobacco plants
2 *Helichrysum petiolatum*
2 white border carnations
2 white lobelias
1-2 white pelargoniums

Most summer window boxes can be planted up in late spring. However, do not put out half-hardy plants until the risk of frost is over.

1 Bring together the plants and other items needed to plant up your window box. Place large or heavy window boxes in their final position before planting.

2 If using a liner, place it in the window box and in the bottom lay coarse material such as expanded clay granules, as used here, or old crocks, to prevent drainage holes becoming blocked. When there is no liner, simply place the granules or crocks directly in the bottom of the window box.

3 Partly fill the liner or box with potting mix.

4 Knock plants out of their pots and, as they are planted in the window box or liner, work potting mix around them, eventually topping up the potting mix to just below the rim of the box. Do not water the plants until the window box is in its permanent position. Raise boxes that do not have liners on blocks about 2cm (1in) high to allow free drainage. Drip trays can easily introduce the problem of waterlogging unless the window box is raised on blocks.

Below, left : The smaller daffodils are ideal for spring displays in window boxes. 'Tête-à-Tête', growing here with ivies, is about 15cm (6in) and often has two or three flowers to a stem.

Below, right: Nasturtiums, which are easily raised from seed, are often hot-colored flowers of summer but here a soft cream blends with the white, pinks and reds of petunias.

PLANTING FOR SPRING AND SUMMER

For summer displays what is needed are flowering and foliage plants that remain presentable over several months. Many of the plants that do well in hanging baskets, such as pansies and petunias, are ideal for window boxes. Those that are bushy are not so tall growing that they obscure the view or make the window box so top heavy that it becomes unstable. The trailers are particularly useful. The frothing and wandering growth of plants such as lobelias and *Helichrysum petiolatum* breaks over the edge of containers and very often hides it completely. Trailers successfully soften unsympathetic architecture but they are just as valuable enhancing traditional stone and brick.

For spring plantings window boxes score over hanging baskets for they are well suited to the shorter-growing bulbs. The most commonly planted are dwarf daffodils such as the delightful 'Tête-à-Tête', Dutch crocuses and hyacinths. But the range can be extended to include species crocuses, irises, puschkinia and scillas, bulbs that are all the more lovely when seen close up. A mixture of bulbs could be combined with swags of ivy.

Opposite : The range of free-flowering and long-lasting plants for summer makes it possible to create a lavish effect even on a small scale. Here window boxes and a hanging basket overflow with a matching planting of fuchsias, pelargoniums, petunias and *Helichrysum*, almost obscuring the cottage wall.

LONG-TERM PLANTING

A strictly formal approach to long-term planting in window boxes can be a very successful and attractive solution. Shade-tolerant plants such as box and ivy that lend themselves to formal presentation can be particularly suitable for windows that get sun for quite short periods in the day. Pernettyas, dwarf rhododendrons and skimmias will also do well in partial shade. A wider range of plants is suitable for sunny window boxes. Many dwarf shrubs, especially compact cultivars of conifers such as *Chamaecyparis* and *Juniperus*, do not need trimming or clipping to make more or less formal shapes as their growth is almost as tight and regular as that of a plant that has been trimmed periodically.

Another, less formal, approach is to combine a mixture of dwarf shrubs and small hardy perennials of the kind that are often grown on rock gardens. As a way of using window boxes to decorate the house this is less satisfactory than more conventional approaches but for the person who is really interested in growing a wide range of plants it offers exciting possibilities. It is difficult to make a selection that will give a sustained display right through the summer so it helps to include one or two plants with interesting foliage. Aubrietas, some of the dwarf hardy geraniums (for example, 'Ballerina'), campanulas, phloxes, pinks, saxifrages, sedums and sempervivums could form the basis of an interesting collection. The addition of a few dwarf bulbs will give splashes of color in early spring.

USEFUL PLANTS FOR WINDOW BOXES

As cottage gardeners have known for centuries, there is no sharp division between useful and ornamental plants. Many culinary herbs that are valued for their aromatic leaves are also good to look at, mainly on account of their foliage, although some also have attractive flowers. The cottager's herbs were generally cultivated in a little plot within easy reach of the kitchen. The window-box gardener can easily cultivate a miniature version of this plot just outside the kitchen window.

Most herbs require a sunny position but otherwise they are undemanding plants. For window boxes the smaller perennial kinds are the most suitable. A good mixture could include chives, burnet, marjoram, thymes, winter savory and the rather tender prostrate rosemary (*Rosmarinus officinalis* 'Prostrata'). I also like to see some of the larger herbs – hyssop, rue and sage (including its lovely variegated and purple-leaved forms), all of which go well together – but these may need judicious pruning to keep top growth under control. The various mints are even more vigorous than these and the best way to check them is to plant them pot and all. Annual and biennial herbs are also worth growing, especially basil, chervil, parsley and summer savory.

Window-box gardeners who are willing to experiment could try their hands at a few vegetables. The easiest are some of the salad crops such as radishes, lettuces, particularly those such as 'Red Salad Bowl' or 'Lollo Rossa' with attractively colored leaves, and corn salad.

Left : Evergreen dwarf shrubs offer great scope for long-term planting of window boxes. The dwarf conifers, cultivars of *Chamaecyparis*, *Juniperus*, *Pinus* and *Thuja*, are invaluable, the wide range available covering many variations in shape, leaf color and texture, and they combine well with evergreen foliage plants. *Chaemaecyparis lawsoniana* 'Ellwoodii' is used here with ivy and *Lonicera nitida* 'Baggesen's Gold', but can also be combined with flowering plants.

Above : Parsleys, thymes and chives are an attractive and useful alternative to purely ornamental plants for window boxes. This planting includes common thyme, sage, coriander, and a *Lobelia fulgens*. Judicious picking for the kitchen does not take away from their decorative effect and can be used as a way of controlling excessive growth. Most herbs like a free-draining potting mix and a sunny position.

A WINDOW BOX OF HERBS

You will need :
Terracotta window box, about 80cm (32in)
  long, 20cm (8in) wide and 16cm (6in) deep
10 liters (2 gallons) soil-less potting mix (soil-
  based medium would be an alternative)
5 handfuls of sharp sand or grit
5 large handfuls of crocks
Trowel

10-15 thyme plants, including:
Thymus × *citriodorus*, *T. serpyllum* 'Annie Hall' and
  'Coccineus', *T. vulgaris* and 'Aureus'
2 dwarf lavender plants, *Lavandula angustifolia*
  'Hidcote'

Most of the window boxes illustrated in this book are boldly planted with flowering or foliage plants that make their mark even when seen from a distance. A number of smaller plants lend themselves to a more intimate kind of window-box gardening where spectacle for the passer-by is not a serious consideration.

The planting illustrated in the sequence on these two pages is based on a collection of thymes. These deliciously aromatic low plants include one of the most important culinary herbs, several closely related species and a range of cultivars and hybrids differing in leaf size and color (including variegated and golden forms) and intensity of flower color. There is sufficient family resemblance but also variety to make a charming close pattern of small leaves and summer flowers.

A similarly intimate kind of planting can be achieved with a selection of alpines and dwarf shrubs, which could be livened in early spring by miniature bulbs.

1 Bring together the materials needed. Place large or heavy window boxes in their final positions before beginning planting. More manageable window boxes can be planted up on a bench in the garden or in a shed.

2 Place a layer of crocks or similar material in the base of the window box to ensure the drainage holes do not become blocked.

3 Add a little sharp sand or grit to lighten heavy potting media and mix well. Three-quarters fill the window box with the mixture.

4 Knock plants out of their pots and slightly loosen their root systems before placing them in the window box. Plant so that they are at the same depth in the window box as they were in their containers. Work potting mix around plants and fill the window box to within a few centimeters (about an inch) of the rim. Leave a little extra space if a top layer of grit is to be added as a mulch.

5 If you have not already done so, place the window box securely in its permanent position and then water.

OTHER CONTAINERS

Changes in the way we live have made modern gardeners increasingly reliant on containers for growing plants. More and more of us live in towns and cities and we have less and less room for conventional gardening. This contraction of gardening space coincides with a growing taste for outdoor living. Our gardens also have "patios" and "terraces", the language we use reflecting, sometimes pretentiously, a view of the garden's changing role. Despite these changes, there is a tremendous interest in growing garden plants and especially in using them to make outdoor living more agreeable. Plants of all kinds – from shrubs, even trees, to tiny miniatures – adapt well to life in containers, giving the flexibility that can make modern gardening so exciting.

The versatility of container-grown plants is enhanced by the range of containers now available. For the well-heeled collector there are pieces of antique quality, including cast-iron urns, lead cisterns and stone troughs. More affordable are the many containers in terracotta and wood that are still made along traditional lines. However, it is new materials such as concrete, artificial stone, plastics and fiberglass that have so dramatically increased the gardener's choice.

The first containers for plants were almost certainly made of terracotta, a material which many still find the most sympathetic to plants. This mixture of yellow eschscholzias and field poppies (*Papaver rhoeas*) certainly looks well with the material's earthy tones.

Above, left: Reconstituted and artificial stone weather well and are soon hard to distinguish from real stone. This example contains a lovely standard *Argyranthemum frutescens*.

Above, center: Improvised containers can be as attractive as those that are purpose made. Like all containers, they should have drainage holes. The pail containing the mophead hydrangea would be easy to drill. Beside it, in a conventional pot, is an *Ipomoea* 'Heavenly Blue'.

Above, right: Wooden planters are reasonably durable when treated with non-toxic preservative. This planting includes ivy-leaved and zonal pelargoniums, *Helichrysum petiolatum* and *Argyranthemum frutescens*.

Opposite: Once common, cast-iron urns like these, bearing an autumn display of chrysanthemums, are now rare collector's pieces.

CONTAINER CHOICE

When choosing containers there are a few simple points to bear in mind. All containers should have adequate holes for drainage for most plants will eventually become sickly if grown in stagnant and waterlogged soil. A container must also be the right size for the plant or plants to be grown in it. If containers are too small, the potting mix will dry out quickly and the nutrients will soon be exhausted. Plants in small containers rapidly become root bound but an overpotted plant often makes root growth at the expense of top growth. The rate at which potting mix loses water is also affected by the material of the container; a medium in terracotta dries out more quickly than a medium in plastic but in terracotta the root ball remains at a more even temperature.

The weight of a container is an important consideration if you are going to have to move it about when it is full of compost and plants, and also if it is to go on a balcony or roof top. It might be much more sensible to use lightweight pots in plastic or fiberglass rather than handsome but heavy terracotta urns. Stability can be a problem with light pots but also with heavy containers with narrow bases. For any exposed position choose broad-based containers.

The useful life of some containers depends on the way they are maintained. To extend the life of wooden containers they should be treated with a preservative but not one, like creosote, that is harmful to plants. An anti-rusting treatment may be necessary for cast iron. Beautiful though they are, many of the pots manufactured in the Far East and in Mediterranean countries are not frost proof and need protection in winter.

When it comes to looks, personal taste is all. Many gardeners create some of their most attractive effects with improvised containers, almost anything from old wheelbarrows to painted tin cans. If there are none, drill holes for drainage in the base of improvised containers.

CONTAINERS AND LIVING SPACE

In the small garden thrown open to outdoor living in the Californian style there can be fierce competition for the available space. Patios and terraces that are not softened by planting can be very bleak indeed but plants may have to take second place to the demands of leisure activities and their paraphernalia, anything from barbecues to deck chairs.

One of the easiest solutions is to treat the garden space enclosed by walls, hedges and railings as a room in which the architectural features are the only fixed points. Whatever plants are introduced into this space, whether it is a balcony, a roof top or a paved yard, they must be container grown to give the necessary flexibility.

Although many smaller containers are easily moved around, decide where you want large pots and tubs before filling them with potting mix and planting. It is worth positioning these large containers, grouped rather than dotted about, and leaving them unfilled for a day or two while you test whether they get in the way of other activities. Containers will also have to compete with the occupants of the space for the available sun and shade and you may not want to occupy with plants the exact spot which gets the last rays of sun at the end of the day.

Opposite, top : Clever use of walls and rails when planting this collection of bright flowers and leafy shrubs (including hebes and *Senecio* 'Sunshine') has turned a balcony into a garden.

Opposite, bottom : In a small space it is better to group containers than dot them about. This group of tubs, planted with mixed perennials, divides one part of the courtyard from another.

Left : Lightweight metal troughs arranged closely on a Paris roof-top support a living screen that gives privacy to a more open area. Planting includes annuals (*Tropaeolum majus*), herbs (tarragon and fennel), shrubs (*Senecio* 'Sunshine') and herbaceous perennials (*Achillea*).

Above : Mediterranean householders have long known how to transform gardenless townscapes with container-grown plants. The street-side row of pelargonium-filled pots can be a model for many a paved or concreted yard. Petunias and a climbing rose on the wall behind provide delightful contrast here.

Left : Many individual plants make up this spectacular curtain of ivy-leaved pelargoniums. The pots are held in supports that are hooked on to the balcony.

Right : Even without a window box you can have a colorful window of flowers. This lovely and unsophisticated clutter of ivy-leaved pelargoniums, petunias, nasturtiums (*Tropaeolum majus*), busy lizzies (*Impatiens*) and succulents grown as house plants and put out in the summer is delightfully distracting.

CONTAINERS AND ARCHITECTURE

It is near the house that we most want a colorful display of plants and if they are fragrant so much the better. Generally, however, the soil close to buildings is poor. Raised beds cannot be built above ground level because of the risk of damp penetrating the house walls, and digging down to make beds could be a major undertaking. Quite often, too, as when a house fronts directly onto a street, there is no question of there being room for a bed. A row of potted plants can be a simple and very effective solution to what seems an ungardenable area and the varying levels which can be created add great interest to a bland house front. A roadside position obviously means increased risks of pollution but even here some plants, including ivies and pelargoniums, stand up to such adverse conditions surprisingly well.

Well-placed containers filled with plants also provide a very simple way of enhancing the special features of a building or of transforming the banal. The entrance to the most humble dwelling takes on a new dignity (admittedly, easily turning to pomposity) when a pair of matching containers and plants flanks the door. The planting can be changed seasonally – bulbs in spring, annuals in summer – or, long term, such as simple topiary in box (*Buxus sempervirens*). The change of level in steps provides scope for fine displays – a cascade of flowers can hide the ugly edge of an external flight and even steps down to a basement area can be utilized for climbing or shade-loving plants. Pot supports that can be easily hooked on to balconies and attached to walls and shutters make charming displays possible in many unpromising positions.

Right: One of the simplest ways of arranging containers is to set them in pairs. The formal touch of a pair flanking a doorway can raise the status even of an indifferent piece of architecture. In hot dry climates spectacular cacti such as these make impressive container plants for outdoors. In cool moist temperate climates most cacti need winter protection, especially from damp, in a well-lit conservatory or greenhouse.

CONTAINERS IN THE OPEN GARDEN

One of the simplest ways to give a garden a note of distinction is to underline its structure with well-placed eyecatchers or accents. This is often done with permanent planting, sometimes combined with other devices. Container-grown plants can be used very effectively in conjunction with permanent features and very often as a substitute for other objects. For example, most of the garden sculpture one can afford, even much that is beyond one's means, is of rather indifferent quality. To my mind a well-proportioned container that has been handsomely planted makes a much finer focal point than a crudely manufactured and mawkish figure.

Containers of plants can be used singly as centerpieces or at focal points; in pairs, for instance, marking a change of level in a path or flanking other features such as a seat; in series, for example, regularly spaced along a path; or in clusters, perhaps providing an accent in less formal parts of a garden.

Choosing a container of the right size and shape is important. Urns or tall jars are ideal as eyecatchers at the end of paths or as centerpieces for distinctive areas such as herb gardens. A large wooden tub or half barrel might be just the thing for a tiny front garden. Standing the container at the right height is important. A few bricks can be as effective as a more formally constructed plinth in lifting a container so that it pleases the eye.

The planting choice is wide open. A particularly beautiful container might be shown off best by just one plant: a nasturtium or gourd for a vegetable or herb garden, and in other parts of the garden an uncommon ornamental such as the gray-green *Lotus berthelotii*, with its trailing beaked flowers of dark orange.

Another use for pot-grown plants is to treat them as a valuable reserve that can be called on to plug gaps in the open garden. Distinguished gardeners such as Gertrude Jekyll have owned up to this sleight of hand. Pots of lilies or fuchsias, for example, can be simply placed among other plants or even set in the ground.

Opposite : Containers of plants, like sculpture, can provide focal points and accents in the open garden. A stone urn and terracotta pots planted with sempervivums mark a curving path. Such accents come into their own particularly in the barer landscape of winter when their shape and materials provide visual interest.

Left : Retaining walls and steps are good vantage points for containers. Begonias fill the handsome pot above a row of plants that includes the foliage of *Agapanthus* Headbourne Hybrids and a sedum. Make sure that there is no risk of obscuring or obstructing the way when positioning containers on steps.

Below : Scented flowers and aromatic plants give maximum effect and pleasure when they are grouped around a doorway or flank a well-used path. Here pots filled with warmly fragrant wallflowers are staged around a short flight of steps, their flowering coinciding with that of a fine rhododendron.

AUTUMN TO SPRING FLOWERS

Seasonal planting in containers can give a succession of bloom throughout much of the year. For those who are lucky enough to have a reserve area, perhaps in a corner of the vegetable garden, where plants can be held before and after flowering, it is easy to keep up a colorful and attractive display.

Bulbs are particularly valuable for early spring and they often look best planted up on their own. Tulips, however, go particularly well with wallflowers or forget-me-nots when planted up in large tubs. In cold weather individual blooms often last well, sometimes for three weeks, but nonetheless fading plants need to be followed by others just coming into flower. Fortunately most of the main bulbs include a range of species and varieties which in succession will give several months of bloom. It has already been mentioned (see page 13) that crocuses are among the earliest bulbs to bloom, appearing in late winter or very early spring. Two other bulbs, daffodils and tulips, have particularly useful long seasons. Very early daffodils, like 'Cedric Morris', begin flowering in late winter. Some of the best small varieties follow in late winter to early spring, depending on your climate, but there is a succession continuing until the poeticus narcissi flower in late spring, several months after the first daffodils. The tulip season is slightly shorter but even that still lasts quite a number of weeks.

There is a relatively limited choice of other flowering plants for this season but some are of exceptional quality. Among shrubs the camellias (in mild climates) and early azaleas are outstanding. As well as the early-flowering pansies and other short-growing annuals and biennials used in window boxes, there are the taller-growing forget-me-nots and wallflowers, which are highly successful companions for late bulbs such as tulips.

Right: Tulips have the broadest color range among the spring bulbs and their season extends over several months. Early-flowering pansies are a perfect accompaniment to them.

SUMMER FLOWERS

Despite the astonishing range of summer-flowering plants that can be grown successfully in containers, we tend to draw on a relatively small group of annuals and tender perennials. Plants like pelargoniums, petunias and lobelias have indisputable qualities that have made them so popular and so familiar. They are relatively trouble free and provide an almost uninterrupted display of flowers through the whole season, so they are particularly suitable for the really small-scale garden where there is no space to keep plants in reserve. Furthermore, because breeding and hybridization programs have concentrated on a relatively small group of plants, these favorites are available in a wide range of varieties. These may differ in plant size and habit of growth (some may be trailing, for example, while others are compact), in flower color and even flower shape. This is dramatically demonstrated by the cultivars of nasturtium (*Tropaeolum majus*): some are vigorous climbers while others are dwarf compact plants; some have single flowers, while others are semi-double or double; and there is the Alaska Strain which has variegated leaves.

Flowers such as lobelias and petunias have become summer clichés precisely because their combination of reliability and variety within narrowly defined limits gives pleasure out of all proportion to the work involved in looking after them. They are rewarding to grow but it is also

Left and opposite : These photographs show two stages in the development of an ambitious and successful summer planting in a large and elegant terracotta pot. At both stages the fulcrum of the composition is a variegated agave (*A. americana* 'Variegata'). In early summer the cream-yellow and purple color scheme is quietly stated by *Argyranthemum frutescens* 'Jamaica Primrose' and *Verbena* 'Loveliness'. A yellow lily is about to open. Later in summer *Helichrysum petiolatum* 'Limelight' forms a wide skirt below the opulent purple of *Tibouchina semidecandra* and the clear yellow of *Abutilon* 'Canary Bird'.

Above : Staging is particularly useful for presenting a series of star performers through summer, backed by a reliable chorus. This custom-built metal arrangement is versatile but many gardeners improvise stacks of bricks, upturned pots and planks. A sensational orange hybrid lily steals the limelight, supported by variegated pelargoniums, silvery *Helichrysum petiolatum, Chlorophytum comosum* 'Variegatum' (spider plant), *Agapanthus* Headbourne Hybrids, *Lilium regale* and a mophead hydrangea.

Right : Short but spectacular performances could easily be added to this summer grouping of interesting flower and foliage textures, shapes and colors, fronted by deliciously scented cherry pie (*Heliotropium arborescens*).

worth looking beyond them for more distinctive flowers and combinations.

One approach, possible even for those without much reserve space, is to introduce an occasional star performer by way of distraction. Lilies, theatrically aristocratic and seductively scented, fit the bill to perfection and there is a color to suit any scheme. Another approach is to lay much heavier stress on successional planting. A skilled gardener might manage this in a single large container (for an impressive demonstration of what can be achieved see the illustrations on pages 74-5). But, if you have a reserve area, it may be much easier to stage changing displays, with a succession from bulbs in spring to late chrysanthemums in autumn, combined throughout with a core of good foliage plants for the best effect.

Above : Few gardeners are lucky enough to have an architectural niche in which to sit a handsome pot. Here the opportunity has been taken to combine some unusual plants with others that are more familiar. A deep blue *Salvia uliginosa* tops the arrangement, while *Lotus berthelotii*, with orange-red flowers, trails to the base. Those planting a hedge might consider creating recesses in the green architecture that could take containers of plants.

LONG-TERM PLANTING

When growing plants in containers it is not difficult to mirror the permanent or semi-permanent planting of the open garden. At one extreme there are miniature delights, many of them alpines, which look completely at home in stone troughs and sinks, and even less expensive containers. You could start a collection with compact species and cultivars of *Armeria, Aubrieta, Campanula, Dianthus, Phlox and Saxifraga* with a tiny hebe such as *Hebe pinguifolia* 'Pagei', willow such as *Salix reticulata,* or compact conifer, for instance *Chamaecyparis lawsoniana* 'Ellwood's Pillar', as an accent.

A tiny space hemmed in by walls can be transformed into a green and flowery pocket by a skillful planting of climbers, several of which do well in containers. Among evergreens with good foliage the numerous ivies are unsurpassed and, as the step-by-step sequence on pages 82-3 shows, there are ways of training them other than on walls. For me the clematis species and hybrids hold first place among the flowering climbers. The more slender clematis are the ones to look for, including *C. alpina, C. macropetala, C. viticella* and some of the large-flowered hybrids, such as the pink 'Doctor Ruppel'.

Most of the smaller flowering shrubs can be considered material for containers. While some do less well than they might in the open garden, others perform superbly. Camellias, mophead hydrangeas and many of the rhododendrons are

Left: In the search for brilliant flower color gardeners often overlook interesting foliage plants with boldly dramatic shapes. Succulents include agaves – the one illustrated is *A. americana* 'Variegata' – and aeoniums, with rosettes of thick leaves, in some cultivars of rich mahogany. Plants with jagged foliage, for example *Melianthus major,* or sword-like leaves, such as the cordylines, phormiums and yuccas, make fine specimen plants and add distinction to mixed plantings. Many of them will, of course, need to be taken under cover during the winter months and kept in well-lit, dry conditions.

Below : Plants trained as standards, such as this *Lantana camara*, are best planted in a broad-based and heavy container so that they are not easily toppled by wind.

Below : A simple topiary box underplanted with London pride (*Saxifraga × urbium*) makes a long-term partnership. Here, though, the lightweight outer container will be short-lived.

outstanding plants for pots and tubs. Of the most popular flowering shrubs, roses, there are thousands of cultivars and many old roses as well as the more modern hybrid teas and floribundas that can be grown reasonably satisfactorily in containers. But far more successful are the many new miniature and short-growing kinds, the so-called "patio roses", that have been introduced in recent years. A good rose-growers' catalogue will help you to choose roses that flower continuously through the summer and are well-covered with foliage, such as 'The Fairy'.

Foliage plants for containers are a wonderfully mixed bag. The perennials include tender plants, such as the succulent agaves, which take to outdoor living in summer but need protection in winter. The range of hardy non-shrubs extends from small ferns, through bergenias and hostas, plants with handsome large leaves, to tall members of the grass family, such as bamboos. The Japanese maples are the finest of the deciduous shrubs grown for their foliage but there is, too, a gaunt beauty in the winter outline of stems and twigs. Dwarf and slow-growing conifers are making a challenge for a dominant position among the evergreens. Some are very fine plants but, used to excess, they can make a little garden lugubrious and grotesque. They are best combined with other shrubs, including other evergreens such as aucubas and box.

TOPIARY

Since Roman times at least, the art of trimming shrubs and trees in geometric and representational shapes has had a more or less continuous history in European gardens. There is currently a revival of interest in the practice and much use is made of container-grown specimens, which are an easy way of adding a formal note to any garden.

Right: In this predominantly green garden a broad array of container-grown shrubs and long-lived perennials blend beautifully with magnificent mature shrubs that have been planted in the open ground.

Many different kinds of plants can be used for topiary but the classics are yew and box, both relatively slow growing, small in leaf and responding well to regular clipping. Dense growth is encouraged by clipping hard in the early stages. To form more elaborate shapes it may be necessary to train growth on to a wire frame. Although it is not difficult to form your own topiary shapes it takes time. It may be five or six years before you establish even a simple geometric shape in box. Once the shape has been established an annual clipping in late summer or early autumn is generally sufficient. If you are fanatical about clean lines, you can clip in early summer too. My view is that the stage when the shape is fuzzily outlined by fresh growth is as appealing as the tonsured state.

HERBS

If I were forced to make a choice between ornamentals and herbs for container gardening, I would come down in favor of herbs. Most of them grow very happily in pots and tubs, and manage to combine being decorative with being useful. The range suitable for window boxes (see pages 58-61) could be extended to include some of the taller culinary herbs of real quality, and some large herbs grown mainly as ornamentals on account of their handsome foliage. Bay, rosemary and French tarragon certainly belong in the first group, while I would put angelica and bronze fennel in the second.

Aromatic plants of the Mediterranean make lovely mixtures in tubs and half barrels. Some plants are best on their own, the mints because they are so invasive and angelica because it makes such a splendid specimen plant. Parsley pots seem to me unnecessarily fussy; I would rather use them for curious ornamentals such as sempervivums.

Left: Ready-formed spirals and other elaborate shapes in box are expensive to buy but some feel the cost is warranted by the established air they bring to a garden. Patience is needed to train topiary shapes from scratch. Such specimens are the work of years.

GROWING A CLIMBER ON A SPIRAL

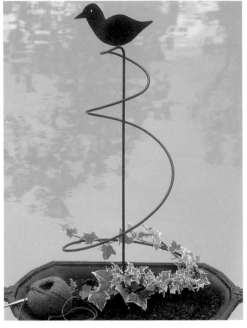

You will need :
Cast-iron container, about 56cm (22in) across
   and 20cm (8in) deep
Heavy-gauge wire spiral, about 50cm (20in)
   high
5 big handfuls of crocks or expanded clay
   granules
10 liters (2 gallons) soil-based potting medium
Twist ties or garden string
Scissors
Trowel

1 *Hedera helix* 'Goldchild' **or** 1 black-eyed susan
   vine (*Thunbergia alata*)

Frames for lax and climbing plants can make an
attractive addition to containers, providing
support and at the same time creating a kind of
modest architecture or sculpture in their own
right. Open baskets of woven canes, as used by
seventeenth-century gardeners to support their
choice pinks and carnations, are easily adapted to

small-scale planting. For a simple arrangement on
a larger scale, a tripod of bamboo canes can be
constructed. This metal spiral is more
sophisticated and is charming whether supporting
the annual black-eyed susan (left) or evergreen
ivy (opposite). The container used here is a fine
piece in cast iron but other heavy containers
would also be satisfactory.

1 Assemble the necessary materials. Place
drainage material in the bottom of the container
to prevent drainage holes from becoming
blocked (expanded clay granules have been used
here but crocks are a common alternative).
2 Set the frame in the container, pouring in
potting mix and firming it around the prongs.
Plant the ivy at the base of the spiral, training it
along the wire and tying it in. Water well.
3 As the ivy grows, continue training and tying
in. When the frame is completely covered an
occasional trim may be necessary to check any
wayward growth and to retain the distinctive
spiral shape.

82

PLANT DIRECTORY

Many more plants than could be listed in this directory are suitable for growing in containers. My aim in drawing up these lists has been to present samples from the main plant categories but, as the illustrations in this book show, there is much to be learned from the example of other gardeners. It is equally true that browsing through a selection of good gardening catalogues can stimulate many worthwhile experiments.

CONTAINER   🧺 hanging basket   🪴 window box   🪣 pot

🧺 tub, planter, large pot   🪟 sink, trough

LIGHT   ☀ full sun   🌤 partial shade   ⚫ full shade

HARDINESS   ❋ hardy   ⚐ half-hardy   🏠 tender

An oblique stroke between the symbols for hardy and half-hardy indicates those plants that will succeed outdoors in many places but may succumb during a very cold winter.

COMPANION PLANTINGS

🌷 Indicates a few suggestions for *possible* companion plantings.

Tulipa 'Red Shine' stands proud in a spring haze of biennial forget-me-nots (*Myosotis* 'Blue Ball'). Those nearby may be self-seeded but linking container and flower bed gives a more established look to a container.

ANNUALS, BIENNIALS AND HALF- HARDY PERENNIALS

ALYSSUM
Hardy annual growing to 15cm (6in) and densely covered with small sweetly scented flowers in summer that are white or in shades of pink and purple. 'Rosie O'Day', rose pink; 'Snowdrift', white. Good spilling over the edge of containers.

FUCHSIA, VIOLA

ANTIRRHINUM
The snapdragon is a short-lived perennial grown as a half-hardy annual. Its spikes, densely packed with flowers in summer, can be as tall as 90cm (3ft) but there are dwarf cultivars, 15-30cm (6-12in), and intermediates, 30-45cm (12-18in). The color range includes white, yellows, pinks, oranges and reds. 'Royal Carpet', dwarf mixed; 'Coronette', intermediate mixed. For window boxes use dwarf cultivars.

HELICHRYSUM, LOBELIA

ARGYRANTHEMUM
The Paris daisy or marguerite, A. frutescens, (formerly Chrysanthemum frutescens), is a tender perennial with daisy-like flowers in summer, the typical form being white. It grows to about 90cm (3ft) but can also be trained as a standard. 'Jamaica Primrose' has large yellow flowers.

HELICHRYSUM, OSTEOSPERMUM, PETUNIA, VERBENA

BEGONIA
Tender perennials. B. semperflorens and its hybrids are fibrous-rooted, making compact plants up to 30cm (12in) high with glossy foliage and many small flowers over a long season in summer. 'Danica Red', 'Danica Rose' and 'Danica White' all have bronze leaves.

The tuberous begonias, if started early in gentle heat, also flower freely in summer over a very long season. The color range covers whites, yellows, oranges, pinks and reds and the single or double flowers can be ruffled, frilled or fringed. Most grow to about 30cm (12in); the pendulous begonias have lax cascading stems and look especially good in hanging baskets and window boxes. 'Gold Cascade', brilliant yellow, and 'Illumination', pink, are pendulous, but mixed colors are available such as Non-stop Mixed,

compact plants with double flowers of medium size.

CHLOROPHYTUM, COLEUS, FUCHSIA, LOBELIA, NICOTIANA, TRADESCANTIA

BUSY LIZZIE see IMPATIENS

CALENDULA
The summer-flowering pot marigold, C. officinalis, is an easy hardy annual, growing 30-60cm (12-24in) tall, with blooms in shades of orange and yellow. The Fiesta Series are compact hybrids with double flowers in a mixture of rich colors; 'Lemon Queen' is tall with double clear yellow flowers. Only compact plants are suitable for window boxes.

NEMESIA, TROPAEOLUM

CHEIRANTHUS
Wallflowers, C. cheiri, are biennials that flower in spring, their delicious scent matching their warm colors. Most grow up to 45cm (18in) but some are shorter. 'Orange Bedder', compact, rich orange shading to apricot; 'Cloth of Gold', clear yellow; 'Ivory White', off white; 'Vulcan', deep crimson.

TULIPA

CHLOROPHYTUM
The spider plant, C. comosum 'Variegatum', has useful cream variegated grass-like leaves up to 35cm (14in) high and sends out arching stems with young plantlets poised at the ends. An easy though half-hardy foliage plant.

BEGONIA, LOBELIA, VIOLA

CHRYSANTHEMUM FRUTESCENS see ARGYRANTHEMUM

COLEUS
A tender shrubby perennial grown for its ornamental foliage, the leaves being strikingly patterned, mainly in strong shades of green, red, bronze, purple and yellow. Plants can be more than 45cm (18in) in height. To make bushy plants pinch out new growth and remove flowers as they develop.

BEGONIA, FUCHSIA

DAISY, PARIS see ARGYRANTHEMUM

FELICIA
F. amelloides is a half-hardy shrubby perennial that grows to 30cm (12in). The blue flowers are daisy-like and appear in summer. 'Variegata' has a creamy edge to the leaves.

HELICHRYSUM, OSTEOSPERMUM, PETUNIA, VERBENA

FORGET-ME-NOT see MYOSOTIS

FUCHSIA
Hardy and half-hardy shrubby plants with pendulous summer flowers in shades of pink, mauve, violet, crimson and orange, often combined with white. There are many variations, some of which are upright, others trailing. Many fuchsias grow to 60cm (2ft) or more but there are also compact cultivars. When grown as standards, fuchsias can be 150cm (5ft) high. Short-growers include: 'Alice Hoffman', semi-double, rose pink and white; 'Elf', single, red and pink; 'Tom Thumb', single, carmine and mauve. The following are trailers: 'Jack Shahan', single, pink; 'La Campanella', semi-double, white and purple; 'Swingtime', double, scarlet and white.

ALYSSUM, BEGONIA, COLEUS, IMPATIENS, LOBELIA, NICOTIANA

GERANIUM see PELARGONIUM

HELICHRYSUM
Two species are half-hardy trailing perennials grown for their foliage. H. microphyllum has small silver-grey leaves with stems up to 45cm (18in) long. H. petiolatum has larger silvery leaves and the stems can trail for more than 90cm (3ft). 'Limelight' has greenish cream leaves and 'Variegatum' is variegated. In summer pinch stems back to control growth.

ANTIRRHINUM, FELICIA, HELICHRYSUM, LOBELIA, OSTEOSPERMUM, PETUNIA

IMPATIENS
Busy lizzies, I. wallerana, are half-hardy perennials that are grown as annuals. The vivid flowers are white or in shades of pink, red, mauve or orange and are borne continuously over a long period in summer and autumn. There are many hybrids available: some, such as the Super Elfin Series,

Above: Abundant flowering over a long season and reliability are two of the reasons why busy lizzies (*Impatiens*) and lobelias are such popular summer standbys. Here trails of purple and white-eyed lobelias unify a group of disparate containers.

grow to about 15cm (6in) but others can be up to 45cm (18in) tall.

FUCHSIA, HEDERA, LOBELIA, TRADESCANTIA

LOBELIA

L. erinus is an early half-hardy perennial grown as an annual, with many small flowers in summer, mainly in shades of blue but there are also carmine and white varieties. The flowers of some have a white eye. Compact lobelias grow to about 20cm (8in) but trailers can have stems more than 60cm (2ft) long. 'Crystal Palace', compact with deep blue flowers and dark foliage; 'Mrs Clibran', compact, violet blue with white eye; 'Blue Cascade', trailing, Cambridge blue. Trailing lobelia is especially good in hanging baskets.

ANTIRRHINUM, BEGONIA, CHLOROPHYTUM, IMPATIENS, FUCHSIA, NEMESIA, TAGETES

MARGUERITE see ARGYRANTHEMUM

MARIGOLD, AFRICAN see TAGETES

MARIGOLD, FRENCH see TAGETES

MARIGOLD, POT see CALENDULA

MYOSOTIS

The forget-me-not, such as 'Blue Ball', is an easygoing perennial grown as a biennial which in spring carries numerous small blue flowers.

HYACINTHUS, TULIPA

NASTURTIUM see TROPAEOLUM

NEMESIA

Half-hardy summer-flowering annual, *N. strumosa*, 20-45cm (8-18in) high, trumpet-shaped flowers available in a range of colors. 'Blue Gem', compact, with sky-blue flowers; Carnival Series are compact, in white, yellows, oranges and reds.

CALENDULA, LOBELIA, TROPAEOLUM

NICOTIANA

Tobacco plants, *N. alata*, perennials which are grown as half-hardy annuals, provide in summer a long display of trumpet-shaped flowers in white, green, red, mauve and crimson. Most of the newer short-growing cultivars, generally about 30cm (12in) tall, are suitable for container growing; their flowers remain open during the day, unlike older varieties, but lack their delicious scent. The Domino Series have upward-facing flowers in many colors; 'Lime Green', short growing with pale green flowers.

BEGONIA, FUCHSIA

OSTEOSPERMUM

Osteospermum hybrids are half-hardy perennials, growing up to 60cm (2ft) high, although some forms are shorter or prostrate, and producing a long succession of daisy-like flowers in summer, which only open fully in sunshine. 'Buttermilk', pale yellow; 'Cannington Roy', prostrate growth and white and purple flowers; 'Whirligig', blue and white, the petals curiously spoon-shaped.

ARGYRANTHEMUM, FELICIA, HELICHRYSUM, PELARGONIUM

PANSY see VIOLA

PELARGONIUM

Pelargoniums, often called geraniums, are tender perennials but are easy summer flowering plants that bloom over a long period. The numerous cultivars are divided into several groups.

The ivy-leaved pelargoniums are trailing plants and the leaves are generally a lustrous green as well as being attractively shaped. 'Galilee', double, pink; 'L'Elégante', single, white flowers with faint purplish veining, variegated foliage; 'Rouletta', white flowers with a red edge and streaking; 'Tavira', semi-double, bright red. This group is especially good in hanging baskets, window boxes and in balcony containers.

The zonal pelargoniums are of upright growth with densely packed flowerheads and rounded leaves that are often marked with a dark zone. Many make bushy plants up to 60cm (2ft) high. 'Caroline Schmidt', semi-double, red, variegated foliage; 'Century Apple Blossom', single, pink, bronze-zoned foliage; 'Century White', single, white; 'Gala Flamingo', single, salmon.

Other pelargoniums worth growing in individual containers are the Regals, with large flowers that are often beautifully veined or blotched, and a number with aromatic leaves.

ARGYRANTHEMUM, OSTEOSPERMUM, TRADESCANTIA, VERBENA

PETUNIA

P. × *hybrida* are easy half-hardy perennials grown as summer-flowering annuals. Plant breeders have developed numerous weather-resistant hybrids of these exceptionally free-flowering plants, which grow to a height of 20-30cm (8-12in). They are available in a very wide color range; there are large-flowered (Grandiflora), small-flowered (Multiflora), dwarf and trailing kinds, singles and doubles. Bonanza Mixed, Multiflora mixture with frilled petals; Resisto Series, dwarf, color range includes bicolors; Supermagic Series, Grandifloras with good color selection.

FELICIA, HELICHRYSUM, TAGETES, VIOLA

POLYANTHUS see PRIMULA

PRIMULA

For best results the hybrid perennial polyanthus, derived from the primrose *P. vulgaris*, is best grown as a biennial. In spring clustered heads of single flowers are borne on stems 15-25cm (6-10in) high. The brightly colored flowers in a wide color range generally have a yellow eye. Pacific Giants and Pacific Super Giants are mixtures with very large flowers; Spring Promise, mixed dwarf plants.

HYACINTHUS, TULIPA, VIOLA

SNAPDRAGON see ANTIRRHINUM

SPIDER PLANT see CHLOROPHYTUM

TAGETES
African and french marigolds (*T. erecta* and *T. patula*) are half-hardy annuals. The african marigolds are larger flowered than french marigolds but they share the same color range of yellow, orange and bronze and there has been much interbreeding. Another species, *T. tenuifolia*, is also the parent of some good hybrids. Dwarf cultivars range in height from 20-35cm (8-14in). 'Lemon Gem', small pale yellow flowers and bright green finely cut foliage; 'Nell Gwyn', large yellow flowers with an orange tinge; 'Paros', dwarf, french, single, reddish bronze edged with yellow. All are summer flowering.
LOBELIA, PETUNIA, VERBENA

TOBACCO PLANT see NICOTIANA

TRADESCANTIA
Wandering jew, *T. fluminensis*, is a tender perennial with trailing stems up to 75cm (30in) long and leaves with a pale variegation. *T. pendula* (*Zebrina pendula*) is similar but with darker leaves. Both are useful and easily grown foliage plants.
BEGONIA, IMPATIENS, PELARGONIUM

TROPAEOLUM
The nasturtium, *T. majus*, is an easily grown hardy annual with attractive circular leaves and spurred flowers in summer, mainly in shades of orange, red and yellow. Climbing or trailing cultivars can have stems 180cm (6ft) long but the stems of semi-trailing kinds are generally less than 45cm (18in) long and dwarf hybrids grow to 30cm (12in) or less. Gleam Series, semi-trailing, mixed, with double flowers; Jewel Mixed, dwarf, semi-double. Semi-trailing kinds are particularly good in hanging baskets and window boxes. In partial shade the foliage is good but there are fewer flowers.
CALENDULA, NEMESIA

VERBENA
Perennial, *V. × hybrida*, grown as half-hardy annual having bright summer flowers in a color range that includes white, pink, red, mauve and purplish blue. Upright kinds can grow to 45cm (18in) but there are also low spreading plants. 'Showtime',

fragrant, mixed colors, compact plants about 20cm (8in) high; 'Springtime', mixed colors, spreading, about 20cm (8in) high. The spreading cultivars are particularly suitable for hanging baskets and window boxes.
ARGYRANTHEMUM, FELICIA, PELARGONIUM, TAGETES

VIOLA
Pansies, *V. × wittrockiana*, are short-lived perennials generally grown as biennials. They grow up to 25cm (10in) tall, making loosely spreading clumps that flower freely over a long season, either in late winter and spring or in summer. The color range is very wide and flowers are often bicolored. 'Majestic Giants' and 'Swiss Giants' are good mixtures for summer displays. The Universal pansies are the most reliable for winter flowering.
ALYSSUM, BEGONIA, CHLOROPHYTUM, HEDERA, PRIMULA, ROSA, TULIPA, VIOLA

WALLFLOWER see CHEIRANTHUS

WANDERING JEW see TRADESCANTIA

BULBS
The shorter bulbs, those up to about 40cm (14in) high, can be grown in window boxes or as an underplanting in larger containers.

CROCUS
A selection of miniature species of delicate beauty and the beefier Dutch crocuses can give wonderful color in late winter and early spring.

The large-flowered hybrid crocuses, known as Dutch crocuses, which are easy bulbs to grow well, have globular flowers about 15cm (6in) high between early and mid-spring. 'Enchantress', violet-purple; 'Jeanne d'Arc', white; 'Pickwick', gray with purple stripes; and 'Yellow Mammoth', rich yellow, are all to be recommended.

A late-winter species is *C. chrysanthus*, which grows to 7.5cm (3in). Cultivars include: 'Blue Pearl', pale blue with a yellow throat; 'Cream Beauty', cream with a yellow throat; 'E.A. Bowles', rich yellow with bronze markings outside; 'Snow Bunting', white with purple markings; and 'Zwanenburg Bronze', dark orange with purple-brown markings.
CYCLAMEN, GALANTHUS, IRIS, MUSCARI, NARCISSUS, SCILLA

Above : *Lilium* 'Connecticut King' is one of the modern hybrids derived from the Asiatic species lilies. Its clear lemon-yellow flowers make a spectacular contribution to the summer garden and the plant needs careful placing.

HARDY CYCLAMEN
There are several dwarf species with pink, crimson or white flowers and attractive leaves that are prettily marked with silver. *C. hederifolium*, 15cm (6in), flowers in early to mid-autumn, the ivy-like leaves developing after the flowers.
CROCUS, GALANTHUS

DAFFODIL see NARCISSUS

GALANTHUS
Snowdrops show a strong family resemblance between species but enthusiasts delight in the detailed variation of their nodding white and green flowers. They range in height from 12-20cm (5-8in) and, with a few exceptions, they flower from late winter to early spring. Snowdrops are ideal plants for naturalizing but it is worth growing the more expensive selections of the common snowdrop, *G. nivalis*, in pots.
CROCUS, CYCLAMEN, ERICA, IRIS, PRIMULA

GRAPE HYACINTH see MUSCARI

HYACINTH see HYACINTHUS

HYACINTHUS
A long history of breeding has produced many cultivars of *H. orientalis* in a color range that includes white, blues, yellows, pinks and near reds. The stout stems, sometimes more than 30cm (12in) tall, are tighly packed with single or double waxy flowers that are heavily scented. Most flower in mid-spring: 'Carnegie', white, early-flowering, compact; 'City of Haarlem', pale yellow and late; 'Madame Sophie', double, white; 'Ostara', deep blue, early; 'Pink Pearl', carmine-pink, early.
🌱 MYOSOTIS, NARCISSUS, PRIMULA, TULIPA

IRIS
Several miniature bulbous irises that flower in late winter or early spring have remarkably robust flowers that stand up well to cold and rough weather: *I. danfordiae*, 10cm (4in), thick-set lemon-yellow flowers lightly spotted with green; *I. histrioides* 'Major', 10cm (4in), vivid blue with an orange crest; *I. reticulata*, up to 20cm (8in) high, graceful blue flowers, generally marked gold and white, its cultivars include: 'Cantab', pale blue with orange markings; 'Harmony', sky-blue with yellow markings; and 'J.S. Dijt', reddish-purple with yellow markings.
🌱 CROCUS, GALANTHUS, PRIMULA, SCILLA

LILIUM
There are few plants suitable for containers that can match the sumptuous effect of lilies. Some have trumpet flowers, others have a Turk's-cap shape, with hanging flowers and upturned petals, and many modern hybrids have wide upward-facing flowers. For those that are stem-rooting a depth of at least 20cm (8in) to the top of the bulb is essential.
The following is a tiny selection from the vast range of hybrid lilies, most of which flower in mid-summer: 'Connecticut King', up to 120cm (4ft), strong lemon-yellow flowers, upward facing and with nicely turned-back petals; 'Enchantment', up to 120cm (4ft), wide upturned flowers of brilliant orange-red; 'Liliput', 45cm (18in), upward-facing flowers that are rich orange with darker speckling; 'Stargazer', 90-120cm (3-4ft), upward facing crimson flowers that are edged with white.

Among many fine species two are outstanding container subjects: *L. regale*, 90-150cm (3-5ft), strongly fragrant white trumpets, yellow throated and maroon on the outside, in early or mid-summer, stem-rooting; *L. speciosum*, 150cm (5ft) or more, large fragrant white flowers spotted and marked with crimson, the petals turned back at the tips and wavy edged, stem-rooting, best started in a cool greenhouse.
🌱 BEST ALONE

LILY see LILIUM

MUSCARI
Grape hyacinths make an eye-catching blue accent in the second half of spring. *M. armeniacum*, 25cm (10in), has sturdy stems that carry densely packed heads of flowers that are deep blue with a white rim.
🌱 CROCUS, NARCISSUS

NARCISSUS
Daffodils are among the most dependable spring bulbs and by planting several cultivars, preferably separately, it is possible to have a succession of flowers over three months. The trumpet, cupped and multi-headed cultivars listed below are short or of medium height and most are fragrant.
'February Gold' 30cm (12in), rich yellow trumpet, paler swept-back petals, early spring rather than late winter; 'Hawera', 20cm (8in), small bright yellow flowers with hanging cups and swept-back petals, three or more to a stem, in late spring; 'Jack Snipe', 20cm (8in), orange-yellow cup and creamy-white swept-back petals in early spring; 'Liberty Bells', 30cm (12in), three or more hanging flowers to a stem in mid-spring; 'Jenny', 30cm (12in), creamy trumpet and paler petals, early spring; 'Tête-à-Tête', 15cm (6in), two or more flowers are carried on each stem, cup a deep yellow and petals somewhat paler, late winter or early spring; 'Topolino', 30cm (12in), yellow trumpet and creamy petals, early to mid-spring; 'Trevithian', 35cm (14in), sweetly scented jonquil with several small and elegant buttercup-yellow flowers to a stem, mid-spring.
🌱 CROCUS, MUSCARI, ERICA

SCILLA
Few flowers of early spring can match the squills for the brilliance of their blue. *S. sibirica*, 10cm (4in),

is the most commonly grown and 'Spring Beauty' is large and a particularly vivid blue.
🌱 CROCUS, GALANTHUS, IRIS

SNOWDROP see GALANTHUS

TULIPA
Tulips are the showiest of the spring bulbs, species and hybrids providing brilliant color from early to late spring.
The species are mainly short-growing tulips of great charm and the two listed are easy plants: *T. clusiana*, the lady tulip, 25cm (10in), mid-spring flowers with crimson-pink vertical bands overlaying white; *T. tarda*, 15cm (6in), in early spring three to five flowers per bulb, yellow-centered but with striking white tips.
The following are short to medium, all grow to a height of between 20-30cm (8-12in) and flower between early and mid-spring: 'Concerto', creamy yellow with a dark base; 'Heart's Delight', white flushed crimson and pink, handsomely marked leaves; 'Red Riding Hood', brilliant scarlet-red with black center, leaves striped maroon; 'Shakespeare', salmon mixed with scarlet and yellow.
The following are medium to tall, grow to between 35-50cm (14-20in) and flower between mid- and late spring: 'Angélique', double, pink; 'Couleur Cardinal', dark red tinged purple; 'Stresa', golden-yellow flowers with orange-red vertical bands; 'West Point', a lily-flowered tulip with pointed petals turned back at the tips, clear yellow; 'White Emperor', milky white with a yellow center.
🌱 CHEIRANTHUS, HYACINTHUS, PRIMULA, VIOLA

SHRUBS AND CLIMBERS

This list includes roses and dwarf or compact conifers. Unless stated otherwise, the following require ordinary loam-based potting mix.

ACER
The many cultivars of Japanese maple, *A. palmatum*, are beautiful deciduous trees, most of them suitable for containers in a sheltered position and grown in this way they rarely exceed 150cm (5ft). An example with an attractive weeping habit is *A. palmatum* 'Dissectum Atropurpureum'. The feathery finely divided leaves, maroon in spring and more green in summer, turn brilliant red in autumn. Lime-free potting mix.
🌱 BEST ALONE

AUCUBA

The spotted laurel, *A. japonica*, is an easy evergreen and in many of the named forms, such as 'Maculata' (female) and 'Picturata' (male), the leaves are boldly spotted or mottled in yellow. Female plants bear red berries provided a male plant nearby. These bushy plants can grow more than 180cm (6ft) tall. Not hardy in the North.

HEDERA

AZALEA see RHODODENDRON

BAY, SWEET see LAURUS

BOX see BUXUS

BUXUS

Common box, *B. sempervirens*, is a slow-growing evergreen, eventually growing to 3m (10ft) but easily kept smaller. Ideal for topiary.

HEDERA

CAMELLIA

Evergreens with handsome glossy leaves and showy flowers in late winter or spring. The hardiest and best for containers are the *C.* × *williamsii* hybrids, which grow to between 90-180cm (3-6ft), although taller in the open garden. 'Anticipation', peony form, crimson; 'Donation', semi-double, light pink; 'St Ewe', large single, pink; 'Spring Festival', small double, pink. Acid potting mix, plenty of moisture. Not hardy in the North.

BEST ALONE

CHAMAECYPARIS

Evergreen conifers, including some dwarf and slow-growers. *C. lawsoniana* cultivars include 'Ellwood's Pillar', about 90cm (3ft), blue-gray column of feathery foliage; 'Minima Aurea', about 60cm (2ft), a dense cone that remains bright yellow all year; *C. obtusa* 'Nana Gracilis', up to 75cm (30in), foliage in dark green sprays; *C. pisifera* 'Boulevard', up to 120cm (4ft), a pyramid of silver-blue foliage.

CROCUS, ERICA

CLEMATIS

Some of the less vigorous clematis are suitable for containers. They can be trained up supports such as trellis but they are often even more beautiful when allowed to trail from a tall pot. They do best when allowed to grow into sunlight but with the container in shade or partial shade.

The following three species are rewarding: *C. alpina*, up to 180cm (6ft), deciduous, violet-blue flowers in the second half of spring; *C. macropetala*, up to 3m (10ft), deciduous, nodding dark blue flowers in late spring or early summer, the variety 'Maidwell Hall' being especially good; *C. viticella*, up to 3m (10ft), deciduous, flowering in the second half of summer and autumn, white in 'Alba Luxurians', rich purple in 'Royal Velours'.

Some of the large-flowered deciduous hybrids, such as the following, are also worth trying: 'Beauty of Worcester', to 3m (10ft), violet-blue, early to mid-summer; 'Doctor Ruppel', to 3m (10ft), pink with carmine bar, summer; 'Lady Northcliffe', to 3m (10ft), lavender-blue, summer and early autumn.

BEST ALONE

CONIFERS see CHAMAECYPARIS, JUNIPERUS, THUJA

ERICA

The heaths offer a good range of foliage color (from green through orange and yellow to bronze) and flowering season, the winter- and spring-flowering kinds being especially useful. The flowers are white or in shades of pink or purple. Cultivars of *E. carnea*, up to 30cm (12in), early spring flowering, lime tolerant. *E. cinerea* cultivars, up to 30cm (12in), summer flowering, not lime tolerant. Cultivars of *E.* × *darleyensis*, up to 60cm (2ft) in height and 90cm (3ft) in spread, winter and spring flowering, lime tolerant.

CHAMAECYPARIS, GALANTHUS, JUNIPERUS, NARCISSUS, PERNETTYA, PICEA, SKIMMIA, RHODODENDRON

EUONYMUS

The evergreen *E. fortunei* has many good variegated cultivars that are easy to grow. They tend to be spreading plants, up to 60cm (2ft) but taller with a support, for many have a tendency to climb. 'Emerald Gaiety', silver and green; 'Emerald 'n' Gold', gold and green, with darker coloring in winter; 'Silver Queen', cream and green.

BERGENIA, HEUCHERA

FATSIA

The evergreen *F. japonica* is an erect shrub, capable of growing to 3m (10ft) or more, with large glossy leaves divided into seven or more lobes. In autumn there are panicles of cream flowers. Not hardy in the North.

BERGENIA, HEDERA

HEATH see ERICA

HEBE

Evergreen shrubs, some, including the whipcords (with cypress-like leaves), are grown mainly for their foliage, but most have interesting flowers, in white or shades of pink, blue or purple. *H. armstrongii*, up to 45cm (18in), a whipcord hebe with golden green leaves, small white flowers in summer. 'Carl Teschner', up to 30cm (12in), grey-green leaves, violet-blue flowers in summer. *H. pinguifolia* 'Pagei', 30cm (12in), silver-gray foliage and white flowers in late spring and early summer.

AJUGA, GERANIUM, HOUTTUYNIA

HEDERA

The English ivy, *H. helix*, is an easy evergreen trailing and self-clinging climbing plant that will thrive in almost any situation. Mature plants can reach a height of 9m (30ft) but trailing specimens can be kept low even though the stems may be more than 1m (3ft) long. There are many cultivars and among the most useful for mixing with other plants or for growing alone are those with white, cream or yellow variegations. 'Glacier' is in white and shades of green while 'Goldheart' has an irregular yellow splash in a dark green leaf.

AUCUBA, BUXUS, FATSIA, SKIMMIA, VIOLA

HYDRANGEA

The mophead hydrangeas or Hortensias, *H. macrophylla*, are deciduous shrubs. They grow to about 150cm (5ft) and in late summer and autumn carry large dome-shaped flowerheads, the flowers in whites or shades of blue and pink. 'Générale Vicomtesse de Vibraye', rose pink or sky blue; 'Madame Emile Mouillière', white. A sheltered position and rich, moisture-retentive potting mix are essential. Blue hydrangeas will turn pink in alkaline conditions, while many pink cultivars turn purplish blue on acid or neutral soils.

BEST ALONE

JUNIPERUS

Evergreen conifers including dwarf and slow-growing varieties. *J. chinensis* 'Aurea', up to 150cm (5ft), gold foliage, becoming conical with age. *J. communis* 'Compressa', dwarf green column to 45cm (18in). *J. squamata* 'Blue Star', compact bush to 45cm (18in), metallic-blue foliage.

ERICA

LAUREL, SPOTTED see AUCUBA

LAURUS

Sweet bay, *L. nobilis*, is an evergreen with aromatic leaves that is capable of growing to tree-like proportions but is easily trained as a mophead standard or pyramid from 150-300cm (5-10ft) high. Not hardy in the North.

BEST ALONE

Above : This splendid sweet bay (*Laurus nobilis*), trained as a standard, is an unusual centerpiece for a table designed for outdoor entertaining. Its formal shape and evergreen habit ensure it looks equally good in winter or summer.

LAVANDULA

The lavenders are evergreen shrubs, ranging in height from 30-90cm (1-3ft), with spikes of blue flowers in summer, in some varieties strongly scented. *L. angustifolia* 'Hidcote', violet-blue, up to 30cm (12in); 'Munstead', up to 45cm (18in), mauve-blue.

HELIANTHEMUM, THYME, ROSA, RUE, SAGE

LAVENDER see LAVANDULA

MAPLE see ACER

PERNETTYA

Evergreen wiry shrubs up to 90 cm (3ft) high, grown mainly for their colorful berries, which may last through the winter. To every three berrying forms grows a male plant of *P. mucronata* to ensure pollination. Cultivars include: 'Mother of Pearl', silvery pink berries; 'Signal', deep red berries; 'Snow White', white berries. Lime-free potting mix.

ERICA, PIERIS, RHODODENDRON

PIERIS

Compact evergreen, generally 150-180cm (5-6ft) tall, with drooping sprays of waxy white flowers in spring. Some have vividly colored young foliage: 'Firecrest', young foliage red; 'Forest Flame', young foliage changing from red to pink and then creamy white before turning green. Grow in a sheltered position. Lime-free potting mix.

PERNETTYA

RHODODENDRON

There are numerous rhododendrons and azaleas of dwarf size or compact growth suitable for containers. The evergreen *R. yakushimanum* and its hybrids are outstanding, with a dome shape up to 60cm (2ft) high and 90cm (3ft) across. The following flower in late spring or early summer: 'Hydon Dawn', pink; 'Golden Torch', salmon pink in bud, yellow in flower; 'Silver Sixpence', cream with lemon spots. Other evergreen rhododendron hybrids of compact growth are: 'Bluebird', 90cm (3ft), lavender-blue flowers in mid- to late spring; *R. × cilpinense*, 90cm (3ft), pale pink flushed rose in early spring; and 'Elizabeth', to 120cm (4ft), scarlet flowers in late spring. The evergreen and slightly tender Kurume azaleas, which need to be sheltered from cold wind and early-morning sun, grow to a height of 120cm (4ft)

and flower profusely in spring. These include: 'Hinodegiri', scarlet; 'Hinomayo', pink; and 'Velvet Gown', purplish blue. Grow rhododendrons and azaleas in a sheltered position. All require acid potting mix.

ERICA, PERNETTYA

ROSA

Although many roses can be grown in containers, the most suitable are the miniature and patio roses. The miniatures grow to about 30cm (12in) but the patio roses can be more than twice this height. There are many new introductions each year. Miniature roses: 'Baby Masquerade', yellow and pinkish red; 'Cinderella', blush pink; 'Magic Carousel', white; 'Perla de Alcanada', crimson. Patio roses: 'Bright Smile', yellow; 'Fairy Damsel', deep red; 'Gentle Touch', soft pink; 'Sweet Magic', gold and peachy orange.

ALCHEMILLA, DIANTHUS, LAVANDULA, VIOLA

SKIMMIA

The evergreen *S. japonica* has a height and spread of about 90cm (3ft), with male and female flowers borne on separate plants in spring. Female plants that have been pollinated carry large crops of bright red berries throughout the winter. 'Foremanii', female, carries large bunches of berries; 'Rubella', male, has pink flowers that are attractively red in bud. The leaves are pale green and leathery.

ERICA, HEDERA

THUJA

Evergreen conifers, including dwarf and slow-growing cultivars. *T. occidentalis* 'Rheingold', up to 90cm (3ft), broad cone of dense old-gold foliage with copper tones in winter; *T. orientalis* 'Aurea Nana', to 75cm (30in) or more, dense bush of oval outline, golden green.

AJUGA, ERICA

YUCCA

Evergreens forming clumps 75cm (30in) high of sword-shaped leaves. In late summer stems up to 180cm (6ft) tall carry clusters of bell-shaped creamy flowers. There are good variegated cultivars, including *Y. filamentosa* 'Variegata' whose leaves are edged with broad, creamy-white margins. Grow in sheltered position.

BEST ALONE

HARDY PERENNIALS

Although hardy perennials are generally grown in the open garden, many do well in containers and those that combine good foliage and flowers are particularly valuable. It is worth starting with good-sized plants. Those who have a garden from which plants can be taken should experiment with a much wider range than is covered here.

AFRICAN LILY see AGAPANTHUS

AGAPANTHUS 🪣 ○ ✳

The african lilies form clumps of strap-shaped leaves and in late summer strong stems 60-90cm (2-3ft) tall carry heads of funnel-shaped flowers in shades of blue or white. The most reliable are the Headbourne Hybrids. Not hardy in the North.

🪴 BEST ALONE

AJUGA 🪴🌱🪣 ○ ◑ ● ✳

Selected forms of the common bugle, *A. reptans*, have attractively colored foliage. 'Burgundy Glow', wine-red with greens and cream; 'Purpurea', deep purple. All are easy to grow, making spreading mats of foliage and in late spring producing spikes of blue flowers about 10cm (4in) high.

🪴 HEBE, HEUCHERA, THUJA

ALCHEMILLA 🪴🌱🪣 ○ ◑ ● ✳

Lady's mantle, *A. mollis*, has rounded fans of soft green leaves covered in fine silky hairs that hold water in glistening drops. In early to mid-summer there are sprays of lime-green flowers. Clumps grow to 45cm (18in).

🪴 BERGENIA, HEUCHERA, HOSTA, ROSA

BELLFLOWER see CAMPANULA

BERGENIA 🪣 ○ ◑ ● ✳

Large-leaved evergreen, in some species and hybrids the leaves coloring purplish red in winter. In spring there are sprays of bell-shaped flowers in shades of magenta, pink or near-white. 'Abendglut', 30cm (12in), leaves turn rich reds in autumn and in early spring there are rosy red flowers; 'Bressingham White', 30cm (12in), stout leaves and white flowers in early to mid-spring.

🪴 ALCHEMILLA, EUONYMUS, FATSIA, RUE

BUGLE see AJUGA

CAMPANULA

The bellflowers include tall- and short-growing species, most with blue flowers, although there are also lovely white forms. One of the best dwarf species, *C. isophylla*, has spreading growth, about 15cm (6in) high. It is not fully hardy but in summer makes a wonderful cascade of starry blue or white flowers. The dwarf, *C. carpatica*, can grow to 30cm (12in) and has blue, purple or white cup-shaped flowers in late summer.

🪴 DIANTHUS, FRAGARIA, GERANIUM

CRANE'S-BILL see GERANIUM

DIANTHUS 🌱🪣 ⊔ ▭ ○

The pinks and border carnations can be grown in containers, the taller cultivars often looking best when supported in a frame of canes or wickerwork. There are several lovely miniature hybrids that rarely stand more than 15cm (6in) high. Good examples include 'Bombadier', red, and 'Little Jock', pink.

🪴 CAMPANULA, GERANIUM, SEMPERVIVUM

FRAGARIA 'PINK PANDA'

🪴🌱🪣 ⊔ ○ ◑ ✳

Semi-evergreen ornamental strawberry with attractive leaves, nicely cut around the edge, and flushes of yellow-centered pink flowers from late spring to late summer. It grows to 15cm (6in).

🪴 CAMPANULA, GERANIUM

GERANIUM 🌱🪣 ○ ◑ ✳

The crane's-bills or hardy geraniums include many clump-forming plants that are attractive in flower and leaf, the rounded leaves being divided into five or more lobes. *G. endressii*, 30cm (12in), pink flowers in summer; *G. × magnificum*, 60cm (2ft), strongly veined leaves, violet-blue flowers in summer; 'Johnson's Blue', 30cm (12in), blue flowers with violet veins in summer.

🪴 CAMPANULA, DIANTHUS, HEBE, HELIANTHEMUM, HEUCHERA

HELIANTHEMUM 🌱🪣 ○ ✳

The sun or rock roses are shrubby evergreen perennials, some with gray foliage, that flower freely over many weeks in summer. Those listed grow to about 20cm (8in) and have a spread of 45cm (18in); 'Ben Heckla', orange flowers with red

eye over gray-green foliage; 'Cerise Queen', double, rosy red flowers over green foliage; 'The Bride', white flowers with a yellow center and soft gray foliage; 'Wisley Pink', pink flowers over gray foliage.

🪴 GERANIUM, LAVANDULA

HEUCHERA 🪴🌱🪣 ○ ◑ ✳

Clump-forming evergreens with bold leaves, maple-like in outline. Wiry stems carry clusters of small bell-shaped flowers. 'Palace Purple', 60cm (2ft), leaves purplish bronze on the surface and purplish pink on the reverse, tiny white flowers in early summer; 'Snowstorm', leaves with a frosty variegation over green have an elegantly scalloped edge, in early summer dark pink flowers.

🪴 AJUGA, ALCHEMILLA, EUONYMUS, GERANIUM, HOUTTUYNIA

HOSTA 🌱🪣 ○ ◑ ✳

Outstanding foliage plants, with the bonus of trumpet-shaped flowers in late summer. *H. sieboldiana* 'Elegans', 90cm (3ft), large blue-green leaves that are crinkled and prominently veined, pale lilac flowers; 'Frances Williams', 90cm (3ft), waxy leaves with subtle variegations in cream and shades of green, pale mauve flowers; 'Krossa Regal', 90cm (3ft), large glaucous leaves slightly waved at the edge, lilac flowers.

🪴 ALCHEMILLA, HEUCHERA

Above: The white-flowered *Hosta* 'Halcyon', here planted alone, is a handsome foliage plant. Its blue-green leaves have a cool quality which makes it an equally effective partner to clearer greens and yellows and whites.

HOUSELEEK see SEMPERVIVUM

HOUTTUYNIA
'Chameleon', which is a variety of *H. cordata*, has heart-shaped leaves with a showy variegation in yellow, green and shades of red. There are tiny white flowers in summer. A creeping plant, growing to about 15cm (6in), which needs moist soil.

🌷 HEBE

LADY'S MANTLE see ALCHEMILLA

PINK see DIANTHUS

SEMPERVIVUM
The houseleeks are long-lived evergreens that can thrive in very little soil. The fleshy leaves are arranged in tight rosettes up to 10cm (4in) across but often less, and some of the smaller houseleeks, such as *S. arachnoideum*, the cobweb houseleek, are covered by a web of fine threads. The leaves are often shaded purple or red and the flowers, held well above the rosettes, are generally pink.

🌷 CROCUS, DIANTHUS

SUN OR ROCK ROSE see HELIANTHEMUM

HERBS

ANGELICA
Hardy biennial or short-lived perennial, *A. archangelica*, 150-240cm (5-8ft) tall, with handsome aromatic leaves and large heads of greenish-yellow flowers in mid- to late summer. Use moisture-retentive potting mix.

🌷 BEST ALONE

BASIL
Tender annuals of great culinary value. Sweet basil, *Ocimum basilicum*, large-leaved and up to 60cm (2ft) high, suitable for pots; Greek or fine-leaved basil, about 15cm (6in) high, good in window boxes.

🌷 MARJORAM, LEMON BALM, PARSLEY

BORAGE
Hardy annual, *Borago officinalis*, 45-90cm (18-

Above: The container herbs on this tiny New York balcony include parsley, thyme and variegated sage. Positioned close to the kitchen, they can be harvested in an instant.

36in) high, with starry blue flowers through summer and early autumn.

🌷 ROSEMARY, RUE, SAGE

CHIVES
Hardy perennial, *Allium schoenoprasum*, with onion-flavored tubular leaves about 20cm (8in) high. The mauve-pink flowers which appear in summer are attractive but should be removed from plants grown for culinary use. Chives need plenty of water.

🌷 PARSLEY, MARJORAM, MINT

MARJORAM
Tender perennials, *Origanum vulgare*, 30-45cm (12-18in) high, generally grown as annuals. The most ornamental is golden marjoram, 'Aureum', with young foliage that is yellow.

🌷 BASIL, CHIVES, PARSLEY, THYME

MINT
Refreshingly aromatic perennial herbs, *Mentha*, including apple mint (*M. rotundifolia*) and spearmint (*M. spicata*), most 60-90cm (2-3ft). Best grown alone in moist potting mix or in a pot plunged among other less vigorous, spreading plants.

🌷 CHIVES, PARSLEY

PARSLEY
Hardy biennial, *Petroselinum crispum*, generally grown as an annual, 25-45cm (10-18in) high, with broad-leaved and curled-leaved varieties, the latter particularly ornamental.

🌷 BASIL, CALENDULA, CHIVES, MARJORAM, MINT, TROPAEOLUM

ROSEMARY
Evergreen shrub, *Rosmarinus officinalis*, to about 150cm (5ft) of erect or spreading habit with narrow leaves and small but attractive blue flowers in spring. There are also dwarf and prostrate forms, such as 'Severn Sea', which are suitable for window boxes.

🌷 BORAGE, RUE, SAGE, TARRAGON, THYME

SAGE
Evergreen sub-shrub, *Salvia officinalis*, a classic herb of the Mediterranean, with good grey-green mat foliage. Purple sage, 'Purpurascens', and the variegated 'Tricolor', with purple, pink and cream leaves, are particularly decorative. All grow to about 60cm (2ft).

🌷 BORAGE, ROSEMARY, RUE, TARRAGON, THYME

TARRAGON
Hardy perennial, *Artemisia dracunculus*, making a rather nondescript bush about 60cm (2ft) high but of great culinary value.

🌷 SAGE, ROSEMARY, RUE

THYME
Dwarf evergreen bushy shrubs or prostrate creeping plants, *Thymus*, with highly aromatic leaves and in summer flowers of pink, purple or white. Selected forms of the common thyme (*T. vulgaris*) and the lemon-scented thyme (*T. × citriodorus*) have golden or variegated foliage. The tallest grow to about 25cm (10in).

🌷 MARJORAM, ROSEMARY, RUE, SAGE

INDEX

Page numbers in *italics* refer to illustrations; those in **bold** to the directory of plants

Abutilon 74-5
Acaena 46-7
Acer palmatum (maple) 13, 17, 29, 30, 80, **89**
Achillea 67
Acid conditions 21
Adiantum capillus-veneris 44
Aeonium 78
African marigold **see** *Tagetes*
Agapanthus Headbourne Hybrids *71*, *76*, **92**
Agave 17, 80, *74-5*, *78*
Ageratum 14
Ajuga reptans (bugle) 44, **92**
Alcea (hollyhock) *50*
Alchemilla mollis (lady's mantle) 44, **92**
Alkaline conditions 21, 29
Allium schoenoprasum (chives) 44, 59, *59*, **93**
Alpines 61, 78
Alyssum **86**
Angelica 81, **93**
Annuals 24, 69, 74-6, **86-8**
    planting 29; from seed 27
Antirrhinum (snapdragon) **86**
Apple mint 46-7
Argyranthemum 17, *44*, *64*, *74-5*, **86**
Armeria 78
Aromatic plants **see** Herbs
Asparagus setaccus 39
Aubrieta 58, 78
Aucuba 80, **90**
Autumn, planting for 13; planting in 72-3
Azalea 72

Baby's tears (*Soleirolia soleirolii*) 44
Bamboo *21*, 80
Bamboo wigwam *31*, 82
Basil *(Ocimum basilicum)* 59, **93**
Bay *(Laurus nobilis) 10*, 17, 81, **91**, *91*
Bedding plants **see** Annuals
Begonia 9, 26, 38, *71*, **86**

Bellis perennis (daisy) 13
Bergenia 13, *19*, 46-7, 80, **92**
Biennials 8, 9, 25, **86-8**; from seed 27
Black-eyed susan vine *(Thunbergia alata)* 38, 82
Borage *(Borago officinalis)* **93**
Box **see** *Buxus*
Bracket baskets, planting 46-7
Bugle *(Ajuga reptans)* 44, **92**
Bulbs *8*, 9, 13, 26, 45, 53, 58, 61, 69, 72, **88-9**
    planting 29; window boxes 57
Burnet 59
Busy lizzie **see** *Impatiens*
Buxus (box) *9*, *10*, 13, 18, 30, 58, 69, 80, *81*, **90**

Cactus *69*
Calceolaria 38
Calendula (pot marigold) 9, 14, **86**
Camellia 13, 18, *20*, 21, 29-30, 72, 78, **90**
Campanula 14, 36, 38, 58, 78, **92**
Carnation **see** *Dianthus*
Chaenomeles (Japanese quince) 13
Chamaecyparis 13, 58, *58*, 78, **90**
Cheiranthus cheiri (wallflower) 9, 25, *71*, 76, **86**
Cherry pie *(Heliotropium arborescens)* 76
Chervil 59
Chives *(Allium schoenoprasum)* 44, 59, *59*, **93**
Chlorophytum comosum (spider plant) 44, *76*, **86**
Chrysanthemum 65, 76
Clematis 29, 30, 78, **90**
Climbers 82-3, **89-91**
Colander, as hanging basket 42
Coleus blumei 38, **86**
Color in flowers 13, 14, 17
Conifers 13, 17, 58, *58*, 80, **90**
Container gardens, origin 7
Containers, 62-83; and architecture 69
    choice 64-5; in gardens, 70-1
    materials *62*, 63, *64*; sitting 67, *69*
    see also Window boxes

Coriander *58*, *59*
Cordyline 78
Corn salad 59
Cosmos 9, *50*
Cotoneaster 29
Creeping jenny *(Lysimachum nummularia)* 38, *45*
Crocus 13, 57, 72, **88**
Curry plant 46-7
Cuttings 28
Cyclamen 13, **88**

Daffodil *(Narcissus) 8*, 13, *51*, 72, **89**
    varieties 20, 57, *57*, 72
Daisy *(Bellis perennis)* 13
Dianthus 25, 54, 58, 78, **92**
Dianthus barbatus (sweet william) 25
Disease 27, 30-1
Dry conditions 21

Erica (heath) 13, 30, **90**
Ericaceous mixture 21, 24
Eschscholzia 62
Euonymus 46-7, **90**
Euphorbia myrsinites 46-7
Evergreens 13

Fatsia 90
Feeding of plants 30
Felicia amelloides 14, 36, **86**
Fennel *(Foeniculum)* 67, 81
Ferns 17, 18, *19*, *21*, 44, *45*, 80
Fertilizers 30
Flowers, directory **84-93**
Foliage plants 17, 44, 80
Forget-me-not *(Myosotis)* 13, 14, 72, *84*, **87**
Fragaria 44, **92**
French marigold **see** *Tagetes*
Fuchsia 6, *16*, 17, *32*, *35*, 36, 38, *38*, *39*, *53*, *56*, 70, **86**; care of 30
Fungal disease 30-1

Galanthus (snowdrop) 13, 26, **88**
Geranium, 58, **92**
'Geranium' **see also** *Pelargonium*
Germination *26*, 27

Gourd 70
Grape hyacinth *(Muscari)* 13, *15*, **89**
Grasses 17
Ground ivy *(Glechoma)* 38
Growing conditions 18-21

Half-hardy annuals *6*, 9, 25, **86-7**
    from seed 27; winter care 31
Half-hardy perennials **84-6**
Hanging baskets 32-47
    extending the season 45
    lining 35; materials needed 34-5
    planting 36-7; 46-7 positioning 34, *35*
    for summer 36-9
Hanging containers 39-43
Hardening off 27
Hardy annuals *8*, 9, 27; perennials 92-3
Heath *(Erica)* 13, 30, **90**
Hebe 31, 66, 78, **90**
Hedera helix (ivy) 13, *16*, 18, *40*, 40, 45, *51*, 58, *58*, 69, 78, **90**
    training *82-3*; varieties 17
Helianthemum **92**
Helichrysum 14, 17, 46-7, *56*, **86**
    petiolatum 38, *39*, 54, 57, *64*, *74-5*, *76*
Heliotropium abrorescens (cherry pie) *76*
Herbs 21, 44-5, *67*, 81, **93**, *93*
    in window boxes 58-9, *59*, 60-1, *81*
Heuchera 13, 44, *45*, 46-7, **92**
Holly *(Ilex)* 10
Hollyhock *(Alcea)* 50
Hosta 17, 18, *19*, *21*, 46-7, 80, 92, **92**
Houttuynia cordata 2, 44, **93**
Hyacinthus (hyacinth) 14, *51*, 57, **89**
Hydrangea 30, *64*, *76*, 78, **90**
Hyssop 59

Ilex (holly) *10*
Impatiens (busy lizzie) 18, *19*, *34*, 38, *68*, **86-7**
Ipomoea 31, *64*
Iris 13, 57, **89**
Ivy **see** *Hedera*

Jardinières *15*
Juniperus 58, *58*, **90-1**

Lady's mantle *(Alchemilla mollis)* 44, **92**
Lamium macalatum 38
Lantana camara 45, *79*
Lathyrus (sweet pea) 26, *50*
Laurel *(Aucuba)* 80, **90**
Laurus nobilis (sweet bay) *10*, 17, 81, **91**, *91*
Lavandula (lavender) 30, 60-1, **91**
Lettuce 59
Lilium (lily) 26, 70, 74-5, 76, **76**, *88*, **89**
Liners for baskets 35; window boxes 53
Lobelia 6, 14, 14, 19, 32, 34, 35, 36, 38, *38, 39, 52, 53*, 54, 57, 72, **87**, *87*
London pride *(Saxifraga umbrosa)* 79
Lonicera nitida 58
Lotus berthelotii 70, *77*
Lysimachia nummularia (creeping jenny) 38, *45*

Maidenhair fern 44
Maple *(Acer)* 13, 17, 29, 30, 80, **89**
Marigold *see Calendula; Tagetes*
Marjoram *(Origanum vulgare)* 59, **93**
Melianthus major 78
Mimulus (monkey flower) *14*, *35*
Mint *(Mentha)* 44, 59, 81, **93**
Moisture loving plants 21, *21*
Monkey flower *(Mimulus) 35*
Moss, sphagnum 35
Muscari (grape hyacinth) 13, *15*, **89**
Myosotis (forget-me-not) *13*, 14, 72, *84*, **87**

Narcissus see mainly Daffodil
poeticus 72
Nasturtium *see Tropaeolum*
Nemesia 19, **87**
Nepeta hederacea 38
Nicotiana (tobacco plant) 54, **87**

Osteospermum 8, 54, **87**

Pansy *see Viola*
Papaver rhoeas (poppy) 62
Parsley *(Petroselinum crispum)* 42-3, 44-5, 59, *59*, 81
Parthenocissus tricuspidata 48
Patio roses 80
Peat, and substitutes 24, 35
Pelargoniums 6, 12, 14, 17, *17, 32, 35,* 36, 38, *52, 53,* 54, *56, 64, 68,* 69, 74, **87**
ivy-leaved 38, *48, 64, 68,* **87**
propagation *28*
Perennials, half-hardy **84-6**; hardy **92-3**
herbaceous 9, 25-6, 30, 44, 58, 74-6, *80*
Pernettya 13, 58, **91**
Pests and diseases 25, 30-1
Petunia *6*, 14, 17, 18, 24, *32, 35,* 38, *38, 39, 52,* 54, *56, 57, 57, 68,* 72, **87**
Phlox 58, 78
Phormium 78
Pieris 20, **91**
Pink *see Dianthus*
Pinus 58
Planting 28-9
herb window box 60-1; long-term 58, 78-80
successional **66-7**, 76; summer basket 36-7
window boxes 54-8
Plants, broader range 44-5
choice for growing 24-6
for containers 8-9; directory **84-93**
from seeds *26*, 27; troubles 30-1
Plectranthus 44
Pollution, and siting 69
Polyanthus 13, 45, **87**
Poppy *(Papaver)* 62
Potting mixes and planting 29; sowing in 27; varieties 21, 24; watering 29
Primula 13, **87**
Propagation 28
Protection against frost 31
Pruning 30
Pteris argyraea 44

Puschkinia 57

Quince, Japanese *(Chaenomeles)* 13

Radish 59
Repotting plants 30
Rhododendron 13, *20*, 21, *25*, 58, *71*, 78, **91**
planting and care 29, 30
Rosa (rose) 9, 26, *68*, 80, **91**
diseases 31; pruning 30
Rosemary *(Rosmarinus)* 59, 81, **93**

Sage *(Salvia)* 21, 59, *59*
Salix reticulata (willow) 78
Salvia 77; *see also* Sage
Saxifraga 58, 78, *79*
Scilla 13, 57, **89**
Seasons, planting for all, 11-21
Sedum 20, 21, 58, *71*
Seed, plants grown from *26*, 27
Sempervivum 20, 21, 58, *70*, 81, **93**
Senecio 17, *66*, *67*
Shady conditions 18-19, *45*
Shrubs 9, *9*, 25, 58, *58*, 61, 78-80, *80*, **89-91**
planting and care 29, 30
Skimmia 13, 58, **91**
Snapdragon *(Antirrhinum)* **86**
Snowdrop *(Galanthus)* 13, **88**
Soil 24; *and see* Potting mixes
Soil-less media 24
Soleirolia soleirolii (baby's tears) 44
Sphagnum moss 35
Spider plant *(Chlorophytum comosum)* 44, *76*, **86**
Sprays against pests 31
Spring flowers 72-3
Sprinkler systems 29
Staging for display **76**
Sterilization of compost 24
Succulents **68**
Summer flowers 74-6
Summer savory 59
Sunny conditions 18-19
Supports for plants 30, *82-3*
Sweet pea *(Lathyrus)* 26, *50*

Sweet william *(Dianthus barbatus)* 25

Tagetes (french/african marigold) 9, **44**, **88**
Tarragon *(Artemisia dracunculus)* 67, 81, **93**
Techniques of container gardening 22-31
Tender plants, care 31
Thuja 13, *58*, **91**
Thunbergia alata (black-eyed susan vine) 38, 82
Thyme *(Thymus)* 21, 59, *59*, 60-1, **93**
Tibouchina semidecandra 74-5
Tobacco plant *(Nicotiana)* 54, **87**
Tolmiea menziesii 21, 44, *44*
Topiary 80-1, *81*
Tradescantia 36, 39, **88**
Trailing plants 38-9, 57
Training of plants 30, 81
Tropaeolum (nasturtium) 14, 26, 38, *39, 57,* 70
majus 27, 42-3, 45, *67, 68,* 74, **88**
Troughs *21*
Tulipa (tulip) 13, *13*, 14, *15*, 20, 72, *72-3, 84,* **89**
planting 29
Turbulent conditions 20

Vegetable from seed *26*, 27
Verbena 17, 18, 24, 36, 54, *74-5*, **88**
Viola (pansy) *8*, 13, 14, *22*, 38, 40, *40*, 45, 57, 72, *72-3*, **88**
Virginia creeper *see Parthenocissus tricuspidata*

Wallflower *see Cheiranthus cheiri*
Watering *20*, 21, 23, 29-30
Wigwam of canes *31*, 82
Willow *(Salix)* 78
Window boxes 48-61; choice 51, 53
materials 53; planting 54-8
role 49; types 51
Windy conditions 20
Winter savory 59

Yew *(Taxus)* 81
Yucca 78, **91**

ACKNOWLEDGMENTS

The publisher thanks the following photographers and organizations for their permission to reproduce the pictures in this book:

1 Michèle Lamontagne; 2 Nigel Temple/Garden Picture Library; 4-5 John Miller (Dennis Moore); 6-7 Neil Holmes/Garden Picture Library; 8 above left Jacqui Hurst/Boys Syndication; 8 above right Derek Fell; 8 below left Michèle Lamontagne; 9 Ron Sutherland/Garden Picture Library; 10-11 Marijke Heuff (Walda Pairon Giardini); 12 Michèle Lamontagne; 13 Eric Crichton; 14 John Glover/Garden Picture Library; 15 Michèle Lamontagne; 16 John Miller; 17 Neil Holmes; 18-19 Ron Sutherland/Garden Picture Library; 19 right S & O Mathews; 20 Jerry Harpur/Elizabeth Whiting and Associates; 21 above Michèle Lamontagne; 21 below Philippe Perdereau; 22-3 Jacqui Hurst/Boys Syndication; 24 Jacqui Hurst/Conran Octopus; 25 Karl Dietrich-Buhler/ Elizabeth Whiting and Associates; 28 Stephen Robson/Garden Picture Library; 31 Jacqui Hurst/Conran Octopus; 32-3 Eric Crichton; 34 S & O Mathews; 35 left Philippe Perdereau; 35 right Marijke Heuff (Mr. D. Burgess); 38 Michèle Lamontagne; 39 above Jacqui Hurst/Boys Syndication; 39 below Carole Hellman/Garden Picture Library; 44 Ron Sutherland/Garden Picture Library; 45 above Jerry Harpur (Blooms of Bressingham); 45 below Ron Sutherland/Garden Picture Library; 48-9 Michèle Lamontagne; 50 Marijke Heuff (Mr. L. Goossenaerts-Miedema); 51 Eric Crichton; 52 Michèle Lamontagne; 53 Ann Kelley/Garden Picture Library; 56 Andrew Lawson; 57 left Eric Crichton; 57 right Michèle Lamontagne; 58-9 Marijke Heuff; 59 right John Neubauer; 62-3 George Wright; 64 left Annette Schreiner; 64 centre Marijke Heuff (Marijke Heuff); 64 right Brigitte Thomas; 65 MAP/Arnaud Descat; 66 above Ron Sutherland/Garden Picture Library; 66 below Marijke Heuff (Gardens Mien Ruys); 67 Philippe Perdereau; 68 above Christian Sarramon; 68 below left Michèle Lamontagne; 68 below right Derek Fell; 69 Ron Sutherland/Garden Picture Library; 70-1 Michèle Lamontagne; 71 above right Derek Fell; 71 below right Jerry Harpur (designer: Penny Crawshaw); 72-3 John Neubauer; 74-5 Brigitte Thomas; 76 left Philippe Perdereau; 76-7 Marijke Heuff; 77 right Andrew Lawson; 78 Marijke Heuff (Mr. & Mrs. van Doorn-Timmers); 79 left Marijke Heuff ('de Rhulenhof' Nursery); 79 right Marijke Heuff (Patricia van Roosmalen); 80 John Miller (Martin Summers); 81 Michèle Lamontagne; 82 below Jacqui Hurst/Conran Octopus; 84-5 Brian Carter/Garden Picture Library; 87 Jacqui Hurst/Boys Syndication; 88 Jerry Harpur (designer: Jill Cowley); 91 Marijke Heuff; 92 Andrew Lawson; 93 Jerry Harpur (designer: Maggie Geiger, The Window Box).

Photographs specially taken for Conran Octopus by Pia Tryde and styled by Jane Newdick: 26, 36-7, 40-1, 42-3, 46-7, 54-5, 60-1, 82-3.

The author would like to thank Jackie Matthews, Mary Davies, and the staff at Conran Octopus.